CW00588106

Windows 3.1

THE POCKET REFERENCE

Allen L. Wyatt

Osborne **McGraw-Hill**

Berkeley   New York   St. Louis   San Francisco
Auckland   Bogotá   Hamburg   London   Madrid
Mexico City   Milan   Montreal   New Delhi
Panama City   Paris   São Paulo   Singapore
Sydney   Tokyo   Toronto

Osborne McGraw-Hill
2600 Tenth Street
Berkeley, CA 94710
U.S.A.

For information on translations or book distributors outside of the U.S.A., please
write to Osborne McGraw-Hill at the above address.

Windows 3.1: The Pocket Reference

Publisher:	Kenna S. Wood
Acquisitions Editor:	Jeff Pepper
Project Editor:	Judith Brown
Technical Editor:	Greg Walters
Copy Editor:	Paul Medoff
Indexer:	Sharon Hilgenberg
Typesetting:	Discovery Computing, Inc.
Cover Design:	Bay Graphics Design, Inc.
	Mason Fong

567890 DOC 998765432

ISBN 0-07-881824-9

CONTENTS

Introduction

Windows 3 has been nothing short of a modern
computing marvel. In just slightly over a year,
Microsoft has sold millions of copies of their latest
version of Windows, which has some appealing
improvements over earlier, less powerful versions.
Windows 3.1 has built on the strength of Windows 3
to provide a solid user platform for the future.

Windows is the graphical user interface (GUI) for
DOS, an older and stodgier character-based
interface for IBM-compatible personal computers.
Windows 3 and 3.1 have opened the DOS
environment to an ease of use previously unknown
except to users of the Macintosh.

Why This Pocket Reference?

This pocket reference attempts to present the most
commonly used Windows 3.1 commands in a
manner that is clear, concise, and useful. In
addition, near the back of the book you will find a
Task Reference, a collection of common Windows
problems and their solutions.

This pocket reference is not meant to replace larger,
more complete books. Instead, it is meant to
augment them. *Windows 3.1: The Pocket
Reference* is designed to serve as a memory jogger
or a quick reference. Its small size makes it
convenient to carry anywhere you need it.

Where do you look for more information than is
possible to present in this short volume? If you are
interested in further information about Windows,
the following books will definitely be of interest:

Windows 3.1 Made Easy, by Tom Sheldon, is a great book for beginners. If you are new to Windows, it will provide you with the solid basis you need to become proficient with the software.

Windows 3.1: The Complete Reference, by Tom Sheldon, is the most comprehensive guide to using Windows available. It provides all the help you will need to install, use, upgrade, and live with Windows.

If you also want to learn about DOS, the operating system used by Windows, then the following books are for you:

Simply DOS, by Kris Jamsa, is for the absolute DOS beginner. Written in a clear, concise manner, it provides an organized approach to the operating system in short, easy lessons. Packed with hundreds of pictures, this book is like no other on the market.

Teach Yourself DOS, by Herb Schildt, is for those a little more comfortable with computers, but unfamiliar with using DOS. It provides a tried and true approach to teaching that will enable you to learn and grow at your own speed.

DOS: The Complete Reference, Third Edition, by Kris Jamsa, is the complete guide to DOS. The third edition of this classic provides the most comprehensive coverage of DOS of any book on the market.

All these books are published by Osborne/McGraw-Hill, and are available at bookstores everywhere. If you cannot find them at your bookstore, call 1-800-227-0900 for assistance in locating them.

Using This Pocket Reference

There are three sections to this pocket reference.
The first section gives information that is
fundamental to understanding Windows 3.1 and
fully absorbing the information in the other two
sections. If you are somewhat familiar with
Windows, however, you can probably skip the first
section, or just scan it.

The second section, the Command Reference,
presents the most commonly used Windows 3.1
commands in alphabetical order. Commands
included in the Command Reference come from the
following programs:

Control Panel

Program Manager

File Manager

Print Manager

Clipboard

Windows Setup

Control Menu

Commands are also included from the Help System. The Command Reference begins on page 16.

The third section, the Task Reference, presents common Windows tasks, again in alphabetical order. This section is provided for readers who may have a tendency to task-based learning as opposed to command-based learning. If you ever find yourself wondering "How do I do...," then this section will help you out. The Task Reference begins on page 156.

The beginning of each section explains how the commands and tasks are presented in that section; read the first several pages of each section to understand how to use the Command and Task References.

Finally, there is an index at the back of the pocket reference. Special care has been taken to make this index as complete as possible.

Keyboard commands presented throughout the book are presented in a different typeface and a different color. For instance, if you see the characters Alt-V-S, that means to hold down the Alt key, press V and then S. You don't have to hold down all three keys at once.

What Is Not Covered

While this pocket reference provides complete coverage of common Windows 3.1 commands, it cannot thoroughly cover an environment as rich, diverse, and powerful as Windows.

A conscious decision was made to focus strictly on the major commands that Windows 3.1 users usually encounter during day-to-day operations. Thus, this pocket reference does not cover information about the desk accessories and games that come with Windows. While these are powerful and useful programs, they are an adjunct to Windows, not a direct part of the system. Besides, to do those topics justice requires a larger-format book.

The command structures, menu wording, and illustrations in this pocket reference all correspond to Windows 3.1. While it will undoubtedly be of use and value to Windows 3.0 users, to get the most from this pocket reference, you need Windows 3.1. With all this in mind, let's jump right in.

Running Windows

Windows is a graphical user interface (GUI) that runs under DOS. Many people have their systems configured so that Windows begins every time they turn on their computers. Other people must explicitly start Windows each time they want to use it. This section is for the latter group of users.

The basic command for starting Windows is

```
WIN /x command
```

where **WIN** is the name of the program that contains the programming code for Windows, */x* is an optional mode switch, and *command* is an optional startup command.

Notice that everything except **WIN** is optional; **WIN** is all you really need to enter in order to begin using Windows.

Windows Mode Switches

You can use a *mode switch* (*/x* in the previous command line) to indicate a specific operating mode you want Windows to use. There are two operating mode switches, as follows:

/S   standard mode
/3   386 enhanced mode

/S forces Windows to operate in *standard mode*. This is an operating mode designed for systems that have a limited amount of memory, typically systems based on the 286 chip. Still, your system must have at least 1MB of memory, meaning 640K of conventional memory and 256K of extended memory. For many users, standard mode is the preferred operating mode for Windows. Because it does not allow multitasking (using multiple programs at the same time), the Windows software has to do less. This means that Windows takes less space in memory and consequently runs faster than 386 enhanced mode. While such a decision remains a personal preference, if you typically run only one application program at a time, you should try standard mode.

/3 is the full-powered operating mode for Windows 3.1. With this switch, Windows uses *386 enhanced mode*. In this operating mode, Windows can access multiple programs, provide greater control for non-Windows programs, and use the full capacity of the higher-powered CPU chips. To use this mode, your computer must have at least a 386 chip and 2MB of memory. In 386 enhanced mode, Windows uses all your available extended memory.

If you start Windows without the mode switch, it assumes you want to use 386 enhanced mode. If Windows determines that you cannot use this mode for some reason, it starts in standard mode. Because of this, you typically will not need to use the mode switches unless you need to force Windows into standard mode.

If you do not use the mode switches, you can determine which operating mode Windows is using by pulling down the Help menu from the Program Manager. Select the bottom choice, "About Program Manager." When you do, a window similar to the following will appear:

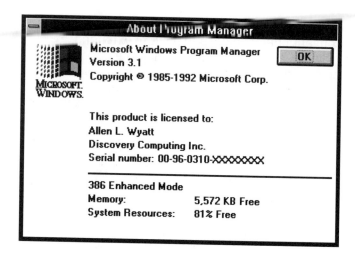

The Startup Command

The next part of the Windows command line is the Startup command. You may use this command when starting Windows_for instance to go directly into a Windows application such as Excel. To do so, you would enter a line such as this:

```
WIN EXCEL.EXE
```

This assumes, of course, either that the program EXCEL.EXE is available in the directory from which you are running Windows, or that it can be found by way of your search path. If not, you will need to include the complete path for the Windows program in the command line.

While you can use the Startup command to begin a program in Windows, the use of the StartUp program group is much more flexibile. This Windows 3.1 feature will be described shortly.

The Windows Environment

If you are familiar with the character-oriented world of DOS, working with Windows may be quite foreign to you. Basically, a *character-oriented user interface* is centered around words and commands. A *graphical user interface*, like Windows, is centered around pictures and menus.

When you start Windows, you are presented with what is referred to as the *desktop*. This is the screen area around which you can move graphic items, much as you would move items on your desk. The two types of graphic items are called *windows* and *icons*. Windows represent work areas, and icons represent files, including programs and data.

Here is what a typical desktop looks like, right after starting Windows:

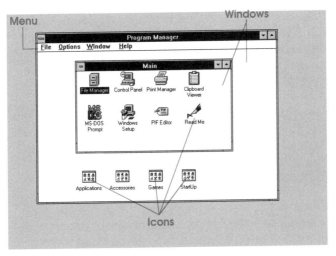

Windows

There are two types of windows: *application windows* and *document windows.* Application windows are created by Windows for programs currently running, and document windows are created by the individual applications. An easy way to tell the two apart is to remember that application windows have menus, while document windows do not.

In the illustration of the desktop you just saw, the window titled Program Manager is an application window, while the window titled Main is a document window. Document windows always occur within application windows; they cannot be moved out of them.

Icons

Take another look at the Windows desktop. Notice the tiny pictures or *icons.* These icons are graphic representations of programs. You can move them around your desktop, if you want, but many times they cannot be moved out of the window in which they appear. For instance, the icon titled Print Manager cannot be moved outside of the Main window. You can move icons freely, but if you move it to an area where Windows won't allow it to reside, the icon changes to a circle with a line drawn through it.

The icons at the bottom of the Program Manager window are graphic representations of *program groups.* This is a special type of icon that indicates there are other programs and files within that icon.

When you open one of these icons, you will see a document window containing other programs.

For instance, the window titled Main contains a group of application programs_it is a program group. If this window were closed, it would look like the other icons at the bottom of the Program Manager window, except that the text under the icon would say Main.

Menus

Application windows have *menus* in them. These menus appear as a series of words under the application window title. You can access these windows by using either the keyboard or the mouse; both methods will be covered in more detail over the next couple of pages.

In the sample Windows desktop shown on page 9, the available menu choices are File, Options, Window, and Help. These are the menu choices for the Program Manager application; this is why they are within the Program Manager window. The choices available on menus are determined by the application program. There is no standard for what they contain.

Besides the application menus, there is another menu you need to be aware of. This is the *Control menu*, and it appears as an icon in the upper-left corner of every window. The icon looks like this:

When you activate this menu, you bring up a special set of choices that affect either the entire window or the entire application. Unlike application program menus, the commands available from this menu are generally standardized. It is possible, however, for applications programs to add items to the Control menu. Thus, your Control menu may vary slightly based on what applications you are currently running. And while the Control menu for applications windows differs slightly from that for document windows, the functions provided by the Control menu are consistent throughout Windows.

Again, the Control menu can be accessed either by keyboard or mouse. The commands available from this menu are included in the Command Reference portion of this pocket reference.

Using the Keyboard

There are two ways you can give commands in Windows. You can use the keyboard or a mouse; for most actions the mouse is easiest. The mouse allows you to point at an object (such as a window, a menu, or an icon) and take some action on the object. Throughout this pocket reference you will see operations presented for both types of users: keyboard and mouse.

If you are using a keyboard, you begin most commands by holding down either the ALT or CTRL keys. You follow this by pressing a key that activates a menu, and then a key that activates a choice on that menu. Notice on the desktop presented earlier the several menu commands: File, Options, Window, and Help. Each of these has a single letter underlined. In this instance it is the first letter of each word. Note that it is not necessarily the first letter. In many cases the second or third letter indicates the key you want to press. You will have to look at the menu choices to verify which mnemonic key is used for a given menu command.

To access the Help menu, you use the key combination A∟⊤-H. You can press both keys at the same time, but it is not necessary. Pressing A∟⊤ activates the menu bar, and the next key you press indicates which menu you want. In this case, pressing the letter H indicates you want the Help menu. When this is done properly, the Help menu appears as shown here:

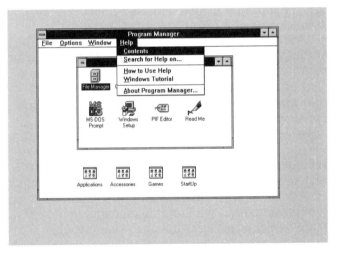

The next key you press selects the menu command you want. There is no need to press A∟⊤ again. If you do, the menus go away and you will need to start over. Simply press the underlined letter. Thus, if you want to access the About Program Manager command (from the Help menu) using the keyboard, the entire key sequence is A∟⊤-H-A.

By the way_you can access the Help System any time you are stuck in Windows. It is a powerful system that will come to your aid in many situations.

Using the Mouse

If you are using a mouse, most commands are started by clicking or double-clicking on an object. *Clicking* means pressing the left mouse button once. *Double-clicking* means pressing the left mouse button twice in quick succession. If you are left-handed, it is possible to change the functioning of the left and right mouse buttons by using the Mouse command from the Control Panel.

For instance, if you wanted to access the Help menu mentioned in the last section, all you need do is click once on the word "Help," and click again on the words "About Program Manager." In two quick movements you have let Windows know exactly what you want to do.

What about double-clicking? A common example would be opening and closing windows. Looking at your desktop, if you double-click on a program group icon within the Program Manager (such as Main, Accessories, or Games), the icon would expand to an open window. If you then double-click on the Control Menu icon in the upper-left corner, the window will close, returning to a single icon.

Throughout this pocket reference you will see instructions to click or double-click. You will also see instructions to *drag* an item. Dragging means to point to an item, click on it, and move the mouse while holding down the left button. In this way you can move things around on the screen.

The StartUp Program Group

One special program group deserves mention before beginning the Command Reference. Windows 3.1 introduced a powerful new feature called the StartUp program group. Any program icons residing in this program group will be automatically opened and started when Windows starts. Thus, if you use a program like Excel or Ami Pro 95 percent of the time when using Windows, you could place the icons for either (or both) programs in the StartUp program group.

Command Reference

This section provides a quick overview of the commands available in Windows 3.1. Because Windows is a *menu-driven* program, a command is basically an option available from one of the many menus in Windows. Thus, each of the commands presented in this section represents a menu choice you can make.

The commands are arranged in alphabetical order, regardless of the Windows application that uses them. All commands use the following format:

COMMAND NAME

Program Name

The command heading shows the command name and directly underneath is the program to which the command is applicable. These include commands from the Control menu, Program Manager, Control Panel, File Manager, Print Manager, Clipboard, Windows Setup, and the Help System. If the command applies to more than one program, then both program names are given under the heading.

If the command is available system-wide, meaning it can be accessed through the Control menu, then the program is shown simply as *System-wide*.

Following the program name is a concise, one- or two-line description of what the command does.

Menu Structure

The first category after the command name is Menu Structure. This section indicates the series of menus you must follow, once within the correct program for that command, to access the command. Each menu name or selection is separated from the previous one by a vertical bar (|).

Steps

The next category is Steps. This section tells you how you can quickly invoke the command, once you are using the program from which the command can be used. The keyboard line tells you how to call up the command directly from the keyboard. The Shortcut line (if any) indicates which keys can be used instead of the keyboard command. Finally, the mouse line tells you how to access the command with the mouse; this typically involves clicking on several menu selections.

Notes

The Notes category describes what the command does, along with any important considerations in using the command, and also gives you related commands. For most readers, this section will provide the most pertinent information.

Tips

Last is the optional Tips category. This section gives hints and warns against any "gotchas" that should be kept in mind while using the command.

There are 104 commands in this part of the pocket reference. (There are 111 commands in the following list because some, such as Cascade Windows, exist under several programs and are listed more than once here.) Following this list, the commands are arranged in alphabetical order. If you don't know the name of the command you need, try the next section, the Task Reference, which is organized by task.

Since this section of the book gives *all* of the commands in alphabetical order, the following list lets you see under which program each command falls:

Program	Command Name
Clipboard	Delete Clipboard
	Open Clipboard File
	Save As
Control Panel	386 Enhanced Settings
	Color Settings
	Date & Time Settings
	Desktop Settings
	Driver Settings
	Font Settings
	International Settings
	Keyboard Settings
	Mouse Settings
	Network Settings
	Port Settings
	Printer Settings
	Sound Settings

Program	Command Name
File Manager	Arrange Icons
	Associate File
	Cascade Windows
	Collapse Branch
	Confirmation Options
	Copy Disk
	Copy File
	Create Directory
	Delete
	Expand All
	Expand Branch
	Expand One Level
	Font Options
	Format Disk
	Indicate Expandable Branches
	Label Disk
	Make System Disk
	Minimize on Use
	Move File
	Network Connections
	New Window
	Open
	Print File
	Properties
	Refresh
	Rename
	Run
	Save Settings on Exit
	Search for Files
	Select Drive
	Select Files
	Sort by Date

Program	Command Name
File Manager (*continued*)	Sort by Name
	Sort by Size
	Sort by Type
	Split
	Status Bar
	Tile Windows
	View All File Details
	View By File Type
	View by Name
	View Directory Only
	View Partial Details
	View Tree and Directory
	View Tree Only
Help System	Annotate
	Back
	Contents
	Copy
	Define Bookmark
	Glossary
	History
	Open File
	Print Setup
	Print Topic
	Search
Print Manager	Alert Always
	Flash if Inactive
	High Priority
	Ignore if Inactive
	Low Priority
	Medium Priority
	Network Connections
	Network Settings
	Other Net Queue

Program	Command Name
Print Manager (*continued*)	Printer Setup Refresh Selected Net Queue View Print File Size View Time/Date Sent
Program Manager	Arrange Icons Auto Arrange Cascade Windows Copy Program Item Delete Exit Windows Minimize on Use Move New Open Properties Run Save Settings on Exit Tile Windows
System-wide	Close Window Maximize Window Minimize Window Move Window Next Window Restore Window Size Window Switch To
Windows Setup	Add/Remove Windows Components Change System Settings Set Up Applications

386 ENHANCED SETTINGS

Control Panel

The 386 Enhanced Settings command controls how
non-Windows programs function in the multitasking
Windows environment.

Menu Structure

386 Enhanced

Settings | 386 Enhanced...

Steps

Keyboard: Alt-S-3
Mouse: Click on Settings menu, then click on 386
             Enhanced...; or double-click on the 386
             Enhanced icon

Notes

This command is only available if you are running
Windows in 386 enhanced mode. If you are not,
then the icon will not be visible on the control panel
or on the Settings menu.

There are two types of 386 Enhanced Settings:
those dealing with *device contention* and those
dealing with *scheduling*. Device contention has to
do with how the system handles simultaneous
requests for access to the serial ports by non-
Windows applications. Only conflicts between

non-Windows applications are affected by these settings; conflicts between Windows applications are dealt with directly by Windows. The three settings governing contention resolution are

Always Warn   This setting causes the display of a warning message when a conflict occurs. With the Always Warn setting, you decide who gets access every time there is a conflict.

Never Warn   Don't ask the user; ignore the conflict and use the port. The Never Warn setting may result in more than one application using the same port at the same time, thus resulting in scrambled data being sent to the serial port.

Idle   This setting represents an idle time, in seconds, that indicates how long the port should remain idle before switching to another use.

Scheduling settings govern how Windows does multitasking when one of the tasks being executed is a non-Windows program. Here you can specify the amount of time devoted to running Windows applications when the foreground task is a non-Windows program, as well as the amount of time dedicated to running non-Windows programs when they are in the background. The time values set represent percentages of the total CPU time.

The 386 Enhanced Settings command also allows you to change how Windows uses virtual memory. When Windows switches between applications, it stores on disk information it would normally keep in RAM. If you click on the Virtual Memory button, you can change the location, size, and type of this virtual memory file.

Tips

Typically the default values are sufficient for most needs. If you find yourself using a lot of non-Windows applications, make some adjustments to see if your overall processing speed improves.

ADD/REMOVE WINDOWS COMPONENTS

Windows Setup

The Add/Remove Windows Components command allows you to configure Windows.

Menu Structure

Options | Add/Remove Windows Components...

Steps

Keyboard: Alt-O-A
Mouse: Click on Options menu, then click on
            Add/Remove Windows Components...

Notes

Windows is a large, full-featured system that encompasses many files and requires a large amount of disk storage space. This command allows you to delete portions of Windows that you may not need, and then add them again at a later time.

You can add or delete Readme files, Accessories, Games, Screen Savers, and Wallpaper files. This command displays the amount of space required by each component, and allows you to delete either the entire component or individual files of each component.

ALERT ALWAYS

Print Manager

The Alert Always command allows the Print Manager to inform you as soon as it detects an error in printing.

Menu Structure

Options | Alert Always

Steps

Keyboard: Alt-O-A
Mouse: Click on Options menu, then click on
            Alert Always

Notes

The Print Manager governs how Windows interacts with your printer. It is a spooling utility, and its use is completely optional. Since printers are usually slower than computers, a spooling utility (such as the Print Manager) allows information to be sent to your printer at the speed your printer can accept it, freeing up your computer to work on other tasks.

This is a *toggle option*, meaning that you use the same command to turn the option on and off. When you select the command the first time, the error notification status for the Print Manager is changed, and a check mark appears beside the command on the menu. If you use another error notification command (Flash if Inactive or Ignore if Inactive), the check mark moves to the other command setting.

Typically the work done by the Print Manager is not done in an active window. It is usually done in the background while you are concentrating on other, more pressing tasks. Using this command causes the Print Manager to display a dialog box whenever it detects a printer condition that demands your attention. This dialog box appears regardless of what you are working on at the time, and allows for the fastest turnaround and most urgency when dealing with printing jobs.

This command is often used if the printer you are using is not near your computer. For instance, if you are printing to a network printer in another office, you may want to be alerted when problems occur.

Tips

If you find dealing with unexpected dialog boxes to be distracting, use one of the other two notification commands (Flash if Inactive or Ignore if Inactive) to set what you feel is appropriate.

ANNOTATE

Help System

The Annotate command allows you to add your own text to the Help System.

Menu Structure

Edit | Annotate...

Steps

Keyboard: Alt-E-A
Mouse: Click on Edit menu, then click on
              Annotate

Notes

While the Help System built into Windows is extensive, sometimes you discover additional tips, tricks, and secrets that need to be kept in a central place. This command allows you to expand the text within the Help System.

When you use this command, you are presented with a window in which you can type anything you want. What you type is called an *annotation*, and is added to the Help System section you were in while you typed it. Those sections with annotations are indicated by a Paper Clip icon to the left of the section name. When you click on the Paper Clip icon, you are shown the annotation.

Please note that you cannot place annotations at random places throughout the text. They are grouped with major sections and automatically placed next to the topic heading.

Tips

You can easily delete any annotation when you find you no longer need it. Simply pull up the annotation by clicking on the Paper Clip icon, and then click on the Delete button.

ARRANGE ICONS

Program Manager or File Manager

The Arrange Icons command organizes the icons in the current window in an orderly fashion.

Menu Structure

Window | Arrange Icons

Steps

Keyboard: Alt-W-A
Mouse: Click on Window menu, then click on
            Arrange Icons

Notes

This command simply grabs all the icons in the current window and organizes them so they are placed left to right, as wide as the current window will allow. If there are more icons than can fit in one row, then additional rows of icons are created.

Icons are not placed in any specific order; they are simply "tidied up."

Tips

Spacing between icons can be controlled through use of the Desktop Settings command.

ASSOCIATE FILE

File Manager

The Associate File command allows you to associate files that have specific filename extensions with an application program.

Menu Structure

File | Associate...

Steps

Keyboard: ALT-F-A
Mouse: Click on File menu, then click on Associate...

Notes

Windows allows you to associate files having a common extension with a specific application program. This association informs Windows of the program it should run if you attempt to open a file that has that extension.

For instance, files with the extension TXT are associated with the Notepad accessory. This means that if you attempt to open a file with an extension of TXT, Windows will automatically run Notepad and load the file.

This feature is very powerful. With it, you can train Windows to automatically treat most of your files the way you want them treated. Windows comes already set for the following associations, all related to built-in desk accessories:

File Extension	Associated Program
CAL	Calendar accessory
CRD	Cardfile accessory
TRM	Terminal accessory
TXT	Notepad accessory
PCX	Paintbrush accessory
BMP	Paintbrush accessory
WRI	Write accessory
REC	Recorder accessory

When you install other Windows programs, these automatic associations get updated. For instance, if you install Excel, files with the extensions XLS, XLC, XLM, and XLW are automatically associated with Excel.

If you attempt to open a file that is not associated with an application, you will get an error message.

When you choose the Associate command, you are shown the document type (the file extension) and prompted to enter or select a program name. If you choose to enter a program name explicitly, enter the full program name, including any drive and path name. You should also include the extension of the program (typically EXE). Alternatively, you can simply select a program from the list presented by Windows.

If you choose the Associate command for a document type that has already been associated with a program, you are shown the current link. You can either change the link or break the association entirely by chosing None from the program list or by erasing the program name.

You can view documents that are associated with files through use of the View By File Type command. See that command for more information.

Tips

When working in the File Manager, you can easily tell if a particular document file is already associated with a program file by looking at the icons. If it is associated, the icon for the document file looks different from that of non-associated documents:

        ◻   Non-associated documents

        ▤   Associated documents

Take a look at your most frequently used document files. If they have a common file extension, then you can use the Associate File command to associate them with the program that uses them. That way, you can browse through the files using the File Manager and have the proper program loaded automatically when you open the file.

AUTO ARRANGE

Program Manager

The Auto Arrange command instructs Windows to automatically arrange icons in a window that has been resized.

Menu Structure

Options | Auto Arrange

Steps

Keyboard: ALT-O-A
Mouse: Click on Options menu, then click on Auto Arrange

Notes

This is a toggle option, meaning the same command turns the option on and off. When you select the command the first time, auto arrangement is activated and a check mark appears beside the command on the menu. Select Auto Arrange again, and auto arrangement is turned off and the check mark disappears.

If auto arrangement is enabled, Windows will automatically rearrange icons when a window is resized.

Tips

If you don't want your icons rearranged every time you resize a window, turn off Auto Arrange, and use the Arrange Icons command when you want them arranged.

BACK

Help System

The Back button in the Help System moves you back to the previously displayed Help System screen.

Menu Structure

Steps

Keyboard: Aʟᴛ-B
Mouse: Click on Back button

Notes

The Help System built into Windows is very powerful. It displays information from a help file in a consistent and clear manner. These help files have the HLP file extension. If, when loading an application program, Windows discovers that there is a help file that has the same root filename as the application program, that help file is opened and ready for use.

When you use the Help System, every display action you take using *hyperlinks* to other help topics is remembered by the system. Hyperlinks are active links between the current Help topic and another Help topic. Clicking on a highlighted hyperlink displays the related help information about the highlighted term or concept. The Back command button allows you to step backward through these related topics. Thus, you go back one screen at a time in reverse order until you reach the screen that appeared when you first accessed the Help System.

The Back command button is not available when there is no previous screen to display. Also, the system does not remember your actions if you use the scroll bar on the right side of the help window. It only remembers screens displayed using hyperlinks.

Tips

If you need to go back more than a couple of screens, use either the History or Contents buttons. The History button allows you to select previously viewed topics, and the Contents button will return you to the beginning of the current Help System file.

CASCADE WINDOWS

Program Manager or File Manager

The Cascade Windows command arranges open windows in an overlapping fashion.

Menu Structure

Window | Cascade

Steps

Keyboard: Aʟᴛ-W-C
Shortcut: Sʜɪꜰᴛ-F5
Mouse: Click on Window menu, then click on
Cascade

Notes

Your Windows desktop can become more and more
cluttered as new windows are opened. This can
make your work more difficult. When you use this
command, Windows rearranges the windows so
they overlap, making them easier to view and work
with.

When cascading windows, they are automatically
resized and, if Auto Arrange is enabled, the icons
are rearranged in each window. The following
shows a sample screen after cascading:

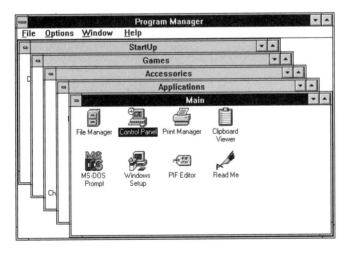

CHANGE SYSTEM SETTINGS

Windows Setup

The Change System Settings command lets you change your system's hardware configuration.

Menu Structure

Options | Change System Settings...

Steps

Keyboard: Alt-O-C
Mouse: Click on Options menu, then click on Change System Settings...

Notes

This command should only be used when you change the hardware attached to your computer system. With it you can change your display adapter, keyboard, mouse, and network type.

When you select this command, you will see a dialog box similar to the following:

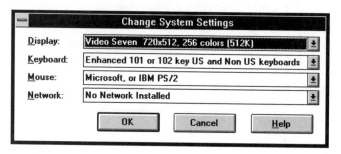

Click on the arrow to the right of the item you wish to change. You will be shown a list of available options from which you can choose the appropriate hardware. If Windows needs to copy driver files, you may be prompted to enter the drive and path of those files. These could either be on your original Windows disks or on disks supplied by the hardware vendor.

Complete hardware setup guidance and instructions are beyond the scope of this pocket reference. For more information, see *Windows 3.1: The Complete Reference* by Tom Sheldon, published by Osborne/McGraw-Hill.

Tips

If you are copying Windows to a new computer, don't just copy all your program files unless the new system has the same hardware as the old system. Windows uses a series of drivers to maximize I/O hardware. If the hardware is changed and the drivers aren't (which is what happens if you copy files to a dissimilar system), then Windows will not work properly. The easiest way to work through this is to go through the Windows Setup again (a new installation) on the new system.

CLOSE WINDOW

System-wide

The Close Window command closes the current window.

Menu Structure

Control | Close

Steps

Keyboard: ALT-DASH-C for a document window,
          ALT-SPACEBAR-C for all other windows
Shortcut: CTRL-F4 for a document window, ALT-F4
          for all other windows
Mouse: Click on the Control menu, then click on
          Close

Notes

The Control menu is accessed through the icon in
the upper-left corner of a window.

The Close Window command allows you to close
the current window. If the window represents an
application program, the program is terminated and
control is returned to a program in another window.

Tips

If you are using a mouse, you can close a window
very quickly by simply double-clicking on the
Control Menu icon for the window you want to
close.

COLLAPSE BRANCH

File Manager

The Collapse Branch command suppresses the display of subdirectories within a directory.

Menu Structure

Tree | Collapse Branch

Steps

Keyboard: Alt-T-C
Shortcut: - (dash)
Mouse: Click on Tree menu, then click on Collapse Branch

Notes

When using the directory tree in the File Manager, the Collapse Branch command allows you to suppress the detail about subdirectories within a directory. A *branch* is another word for a subdirectory. So, this command allows you to collapse subdirectories. For example, compare the following two screens. The first shows the subdirectory C:\BC7 fully expanded; the second shows the same directory after the Collapse Branch command has been used. If it is possible to collapse a subdirectory, there will be a dash, or minus sign, in the directory's icon. If it has been collapsed, there will be a plus sign in the icon.

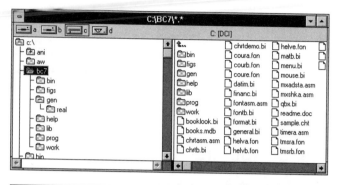

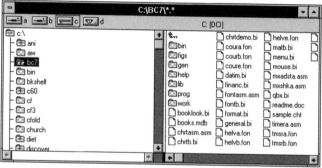

For other commands affecting the display of the directory tree, see Expand One Level, Expand Branch, and Expand All.

Tips

If you are using the mouse, simply click on any subdirectory icon containing a dash, or minus sign. This is a fast, efficient way to collapse subdirectories.

COLOR SETTINGS

Control Panel

The Color Settings command changes the colors used by Windows.

Menu Structure

Color

Settings | Color...

Steps

Keyboard: Alt-S-C
Mouse: Click on Settings menu, then click on Color...; or double-click on the Color icon

Notes

When it comes to displaying colors, Windows allows you to completely configure how your environment will appear. When you use this command, you are given the option of selecting a predefined color scheme. Windows comes with the following schemes predefined:

Arizona
Black Leather Jacket
Bordeaux
Cinnamon
Designer
Emerald City
Fluorescent

Hotdog Stand
LCD Default Screen
    Settings
LCD Reversed - Dark
LCD Reversed - Light
Mahogany
Monochrome

Ocean	The Blues
Pastel	Tweed
Patchwork	Valentine
Plasma Power Saver	Windows Default
Rugby	Wingtips

You can define additional color schemes by clicking on the Color Palette button. Windows allows you to change the colors of the following screen elements:

Active Border	Highlight Text
Active Title Bar	Inactive Border
Active Title Bar Text	Inactive Title Bar
Application Workspace	Inactive Title Bar Text
Button Face	Menu Bar
Button Highlight	Menu Text
Button Shadow	Scroll Bars
Button Text	Window Background
Desktop	Window Frame
Disabled Text	Window Text
Highlight	

Between sessions, Windows remembers the colors you set. You should only have to set them once. However, you are free to experiment and change colors whenever you desire.

Tips

How your colors appear will depend, in large part, on the type of video display and monitor you are using. If you use color combinations that offer adequate contrast on a color monitor, and you later change to a monochrome monitor, you will be disappointed if you find you cannot discern your text or menus. Make sure you make color changes to a "safe" setting before making drastic hardware changes.

CONFIRMATION OPTIONS

File Manager

The Confirmation Options allow you to specify when the File Manager should check with you before taking an action.

Menu Structure

Options | Confirmation...

Steps

Keyboard: Aʟᴛ-O-C
Mouse: Click on Options menu, then click on Confirmation...

Notes

This is an insurance command. Normally, the File Manager checks with you whenever it is about to do anything that could be potentially destructive. The Confirmation Options allow you to modify the amount of confirmation insurance applied to the File Manager. There are four options you can set with this command:

File Delete   If this option is selected, the File Manager will ask for confirmation before deleting a file. If you are deleting a large group of files, this individual confirmation can get tedious.

Directory Delete   If this option is selected, the File Manager will ask for confirmation before removing a subdirectory.

File Replace   If this option is selected, the File Manager will ask for confirmation before completing an operation that would overwrite the contents of an existing file.

Mouse Action   Some File Manager operations are very easy to do with a mouse. If this option is selected, you will be asked for confirmation before the File Manager completes a dragging, moving, or copying operation done with the mouse.

Disk Commands   This option, when selected, causes Windows to ask for confirmation before formatting or copying a disk.

Tips

If you turn messaging off, be sure to turn it back on if you think you may need it in a future File Manager session.

CONTENTS

Help System

The Contents button in the Help System moves you to the contents screen for the current help file.

Menu Structure

Steps

Keyboard: Alt-C
Mouse: Click on Contents button

Notes

The Help System built into Windows is very
powerful. It displays information from a help file in
a consistent and clear manner. These help files
have the HLP file extension. If, when loading an
application program, Windows discovers that there
is a help file that has the same root filename as the
application program, that help file is opened and
ready for use.

Each help file has a table of contents for the file.
This command allows you to access that contents
screen at any time.

COPY

Help System

The Copy command copies the current major Help
System section to the Clipboard.

Menu Structure

Edit I Copy

Steps

Keyboard: Alt-E-C
Shortcut: Ctrl-Ins
Mouse: Click on Edit menu, then click on Copy

Notes

Sometimes it is helpful to see something in your own wording. If you want to rewrite a portion of the Help System, you can do so by using the Copy command. This will copy the text of the help section on your screen into the Clipboard. Then you can use the Clipboard to paste the text into another program such as a word processor.

Remember that each time you copy or delete something, whatever was in the Clipboard before is lost. It is overwritten with the information you just copied (or deleted).

Tips

If you simply want a hard copy printout of the help section, see the Print Topic command.

COPY DISK

File Manager

The Copy Disk command copies the contents of one disk to another.

Menu Structure

Disk | Copy Disk...

Steps

Keyboard: ALT-D-C
Mouse: Click on Disk menu, then click on Copy
             Disk...

Notes

The Copy Disk command allows you to make copies
of entire disks. If you only want to copy files, see
the Copy File command.

When you choose this command, you are asked to
specify the source and destination drives for the
disk to be copied. You can only copy disks of like
capacity. This means that you cannot copy a 360K
disk to a 1.2MB disk, nor can you copy from a 5.25-
inch to a 3.5-inch disk.

> *Warning: Copy Disk is a destructive
> command. It will erase any data on the
> destination disk, overwriting it with the
> information copied from the source disk.*

Tips

Always make backup copies of your important
disks. The time and effort spent making copies will
be repaid in full if just one of your original disks
goes bad.

To copy everything between dissimilar disk types, simply use the Copy File command with the *.* wildcard characters.

COPY FILE

File Manager

The Copy File command copies files or directories from one place to another.

Menu Structure

File | Copy...

Steps

Keyboard: ALT-F-C
Shortcut: F8
Mouse: Click on File menu, then click on Copy...

Notes

This function allows you to copy files or entire subdirectories from one place to another. If the place you are copying from (the *source*) and the place you are copying to (the *destination*) are both on the same disk, and you are using a mouse, hold down the CTRL key and drag the icon for the file or directory to the destination. If desired, the destination can be the icon for another drive.

If you are not using a mouse, you should select the Copy command. You can then specify the *from* and *to* locations for the operation using wildcard characters to copy multiple files in one operation. The source and destination do not need to be on the same drive.

Besides copying files to another disk location, this command allows you to copy them to the Clipboard so they can be imbedded in another Windows application.

Tips

If you are using a mouse and the source and destination are on different drives, you can open multiple windows for the directories on the differing drives. Then simply drag the files or subdirectories between windows. There is no need to hold down the Cᴛʀʟ key in this instance.

COPY PROGRAM ITEM

Program Manager

The Copy Program Item command allows you to duplicate application program icons in the Program Manager.

Menu Structure

File I Copy...

Steps

Keyboard: Aʟᴛ-F-C
Source: F8
Mouse: Click on File menu, then click on Copy...

Notes

For readers who are not using a mouse, the Copy
Program Item command is what you use to copy
program icons from one program group to another.
Select the icon you wish to copy, and then issue this
command. You will be prompted for the name of
the group to which you want the program copied.

Tips

If you are using a mouse, you can accomplish this
task much more easily. All you need to do is hold
down the Cᴛʀʟ key and drag the program icon to the
program group where you want it copied.

Use the Move command if you want to move an icon
into another program group.

CREATE DIRECTORY

File Manager

The Create Directory command allows you to create
subdirectories.

Menu Structure

File | Create Directory...

Steps

Keyboard: Aʟᴛ-F-E
Mouse: Click on File menu, then click on Create
Directory...

Notes

This command allows you to create a directory, into
which you can then place files. When you choose
this command, you are asked to provide the name of
the directory you wish to create. You can either
type a single name (in which case the subdirectory
will be created in the current directory), or you can
provide a full path name of the subdirectory to be
created.

DATE & TIME SETTINGS

Control Panel

The Date & Time Settings command changes the
date and time used by the system.

Menu Structure

Date/Time

Settings | Date/Time...

Steps

Keyboard: Aʟᴛ-S-T
Mouse: Click on Settings menu, then click on
            Date/Time...; or double-click on the
            Date/Time icon

Notes

Your computer system keeps track of the time and
date internally. Windows accesses this information

in order to control some functions. For instance, the Calendar and Clock accessories use the date and time information to operate properly.

This command allows you to change both the date and time. You can either type in new information, or use the up and down control buttons to change it.

Tips

The format used to display the date and time is controlled by the International Settings command. See that command for more information.

DEFINE BOOKMARK

Help System

The Define Bookmark command places a marker at a commonly referenced point in the Help System.

Menu Structure

Bookmark | Define...

Steps

Keyboard: Alt-M-D
Mouse: Click on Bookmark menu, then click on Define...

Notes

Just as bookmarks help you mark your place in books made of paper, so do electronic bookmarks make it easier for you to locate your place in the

Help System. The Define Bookmark command allows you to place bookmarks anywhere you like within a Help System volume. The name you give the bookmark is up to you; after the bookmark is added, the name will appear in the Bookmark menu.

A bookmark does more than just mark a help topic. It actually saves your screen location. When you later return to a place marked by a bookmark, the screen will appear exactly the same way it appeared when you placed the bookmark.

Tips

This command is also used to delete a bookmark. To do this, select the Define Bookmark command. When the menu appears, click on the bookmark you want to delete, and then click the Delete button.

DELETE

File Manager

The Delete command under the File Manager allows deletion of files or subdirectories.

Menu Structure

File | Delete...

Steps

Keyboard: Alt-F-D
Shortcut: Del
Mouse: Click on File menu, then click on
             Delete...

Notes

This command allows you to delete files or subdirectories. If a file has the read-only attribute enabled, it cannot be deleted without first disabling the attribute. For more information on attributes, see the Properties command.

When you choose the Delete command, you are presented with a dialog box that asks you to specify the file or directory you wish to delete. The default is the currently selected file or directory. If the default is not correct, you can type in another file or directory specification.

When you delete the item, you are asked to confirm your intentions. If you select Yes, the file and/or subdirectory are erased from the disk. Note that confirmation only occurs if you have not disabled the Confirm on File Delete and Confirm on Directory Delete options. See the Confirmation Options command for more information.

Warning: Delete is a destructive command. It will erase any file or subdirectory you specify, so use it with care. Be sure you really want to delete something before you use this command.

You can delete a program using this command and still find that the program icon used by the Program Manager was not deleted. You need to use the Delete command under the Program Manager to delete the icon, as explained next.

DELETE

Program Manager

The Delete command under the Program Manager allows deletion of a program group or an application program.

Menu Structure

File | Delete...

Steps

Keyboard: ALT-F-D
Shortcut: DEL
Mouse: Click on File menu, then click on Delete...

Notes

Before you select this command, make sure you have selected the program group or application program you wish to delete. Regardless of which type of item you are deleting, you will be asked to confirm your choice. If you continue, then the program or program group is deleted. Once deleted, it is no longer available from the Program Manager.

Typically you will not need to use this command. It is provided for advanced users of Windows, and is beyond the scope of this pocket reference. For more information, see *Windows 3.1: The Complete Reference* by Tom Sheldon.

DELETE CLIPBOARD

Clipboard

The Delete Clipboard command deletes the contents of the Clipboard.

Menu Structure

Edit | Delete

Steps

Keyboard: ALT-E-D
Shortcut: DEL
Mouse: Click on Edit menu, then click on Delete

Notes

This command is used to clear the Clipboard. After completion, whatever was in the Clipboard is lost, and there is no way to recover it (unless you have previously saved it to a Clipboard file). The destructive nature of this command is why Windows asks you to confirm your actions.

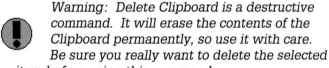 *Warning: Delete Clipboard is a destructive command. It will erase the contents of the Clipboard permanently, so use it with care. Be sure you really want to delete the selected item before using this command.*

DESKTOP SETTINGS

Control Panel

The Desktop Settings command changes the appearance of your desktop, including patterns and wallpaper, cursor appearance, and icon spacing.

Menu Structure

Desktop

Settings | Desktop...

Steps

Keyboard: Aʟᴛ-S-D

Mouse: Click on Settings menu, then click on
                 Desktop...; or double-click on the
                 Desktop icon

Notes

This command controls the setting of several facets of your desktop. These include:

Pattern   Pattern refers to the design used to cover the desktop. The colors used to display the pattern are controlled by the Color Settings command.

Wallpaper   Wallpaper refers to the picture used to overlay the desktop pattern. A graphics file saved in a special bit-map format (these have a BMP file extension) can be used for the wallpaper. BMP files can be created with programs such as the Paintbrush accessory. Display options include centering the picture on the desktop, or repeating an image as many times as necessary to fill the desktop with a pattern instead of a solid color (*tiling*).

Cursor Blink Rate   The cursor blink rate is the speed at which the cursor blinks while awaiting user input.

Icons   This option determines spacing_how close (in pixels) icons are placed in relation to each other within a window. This value is used by Windows when aligning icons within a window.

Sizing Grid   The two settings here control the *granularity* and *border width* used by Windows. The value you set for granularity is used by Windows to establish a grid for aligning icons within a window. Windows multiplies this granularity value by 8 to determine how many pixels apart the invisible grid lines should be. The border width setting specifies how many pixels wide the border is around individual windows.

Screen Saver   When Windows is left unattended for a time, it uses a *screen saver* to help prolong the life of your monitor. Some displays, when left on and unchanging for long periods of time, will damage the phosphors on the inside of your monitor. A screen saver prevents this by automatically displaying a constantly changing scene on your monitor. Windows allows you to control what, how, and when screen savers are displayed.

There are several stock patterns and wallpaper files you may wish to use; these come with Windows. You can also find additional wallpaper graphics from users groups or from bulletin board systems such as CompuServe.

DRIVER SETTINGS

Control Panel

The Driver Settings command allows you to control multimedia device drivers.

Menu Structure

 Settings | Drivers...

Drivers

Steps

Keyboard: Aʟᴛ-S-R
Mouse: Click on Settings menu, then click on Drivers...; or double-click on the Drivers icon

Notes

This command allows you to add, modify, or remove drivers for multimedia cards that can be used by Windows. This includes sound cards, MIDI control boards, and video player controllers. The settings controlled by this command are used by other Windows features, such as the ability to control event sounds. See the Sound Settings command for more information.

EXIT WINDOWS

Program Manager

The Exit Windows command lets you leave the Windows environment and return to DOS.

Menu Structure

File | Exit Windows...

Steps

Keyboard: Alt-F-X
Shortcut: Alt-F4
Mouse: Click on Files menu, then click on Exit Windows...

Notes

When you are finished with Windows, you can exit to DOS by selecting this command. Make sure you really want to leave, as any programs running in the background will be canceled, and any print jobs in the Print Manager will be lost.

When you choose to exit, Windows will prompt you to make sure this is what you really want to do. If you want any system changes you have made (including moving icons and resizing windows) to be saved until the next Windows session, you should make sure the Save Settings on Exit option is selected.

Tips

If you are using a mouse, to exit Windows you can
double-click on the Control Menu icon for the
Program Manager.

EXPAND ALL

File Manager

The Expand All command displays every
subdirectory for the current drive.

Menu Structure

Tree | Expand All

Steps

Keyboard: ALT-T-A
Shortcut: CTRL-*
Mouse: Click on Tree menu, then click on
Expand All

Notes

When using the directory tree in the File Manager,
this command allows you to see every subdirectory
on a drive. It is the same as moving the directory
tree cursor to the root directory level and using the
Expand Branch command. All subdirectories are
displayed, down to the lowest level.

For other commands affecting the display of the
directory tree, see Collapse Branch, Expand Branch,
and Expand One Level.

EXPAND BRANCH

File Manager

The Expand Branch command displays any
subdirectories within the selected directory, down
to the lowest level.

Menu Structure

Tree | Expand Branch

Steps

Keyboard: Alt-T-B
Shortcut: *
Mouse: Click on Tree menu, then click on
               Expand Branch

Notes

When using the directory tree in the File Manager,
this command allows you to see all subdirectories
within a directory. It is similar to the Expand One
Level command, but Expand Branch will expand
multiple levels of directories, starting at the selected
directory.

For screens showing example directory trees that
are expanded and collapsed, see the Collapse
Branch command. For other commands affecting

the display of the directory tree, see also the
Expand All and Expand One Level commands.

EXPAND ONE LEVEL

File Manager

The Expand One Level command displays any
subdirectories within the selected directory.

Menu Structure

Tree | Expand One Level

Steps

Keyboard: Aʟᴛ-T-X
Shortcut: +
Mouse: Click on Tree menu, then click on
Expand One Level

Notes

When using the directory tree in the File Manager,
this command allows you to see detail about what
subdirectories are within a directory. For screens
showing example directory trees that are expanded
and collapsed, see the Collapse Branch command.

For other commands affecting the display of the
directory tree, see also Expand Branch and Expand
All.

Tips

If you are using the mouse, simply click on any subdirectory icon containing a plus sign. This is a fast, efficient way to expand subdirectories.

FLASH IF INACTIVE

Print Manager

If the Print Manager is inactive, the Flash if Inactive command causes the Print Manager icon or title bar to blink if an error in printing is detected.

Menu Structure

Options | Flash if Inactive

Steps

Keyboard: Alt-O-F
Mouse: Click on Options menu, then click on Flash if Inactive

Notes

The Print Manager governs how Windows interacts with your printer. It is a spooling utility, and its use is completely optional. Since printers are usually slower than computers, a spooling utility (such as the Print Manager) allows information to be sent to your printer at the speed your printer can accept it, freeing up your computer to work on other tasks.

This is a toggle command, meaning the command can be turned on and off. When you select the command the first time, the error notification status for the Print Manager is changed, and a check mark appears beside the command on the menu. If you use another error notification command (Alert Always or Ignore if Inactive), the check mark moves to the other command setting.

Typically the work done by the Print Manager is not done in an active window. It is usually done in the background while you are concentrating on other, more pressing tasks. Using this command determines how the Print Manager notifies you if it detects a condition that demands your attention.

After this command, if the Print Manager is in an inactive window or if it is minimized, the following will happen when an error is detected:

1. The title bar at the top of the Print Manager window will flash. (Obviously, this does not happen if the Print Manager is minimized.)

2. The icon for the Print Manager will blink.

When you make the Print Manager the active window, the error message dialog box will be displayed. This is the default setting for Print Manager error notification.

If the Print Manager is already the active window, then the error message dialog box is displayed immediately.

FONT OPTIONS

File Manager

The Font Options command allows you to select the display fonts used by the File Manager.

Menu Structure

Options | Font...

Steps

Keyboard: Alt-O-F
Mouse: Click on Options menu, then click on Font...

Notes

This command allows you to change the fonts used by the File Manager. You can select the font, the style, and the size. You can also specify whether information should be displayed in lowercase. The choices you make with this command affect all File Manager windows.

Font styles include regular, italic, bold, and bold italic. Available font sizes can vary, depending on the font selected.

Tips

If you want to set the font back to the default Windows font, choose 8-point regular MS Sans Serif, and select the lowercase box.

FONT SETTINGS

Control Panel

The Font Settings command allows viewing, adding, and removing system font sets.

Menu Structure

Fonts

Settings | Fonts...

Steps

Keyboard: Aʟᴛ-S-F
Mouse: Click on Settings menu, then click on Fonts...; or double-click on the Fonts icon

Notes

Windows supports a multitude of screen and printer fonts. It comes with a sizeable collection of fonts that can be used in Windows applications (such as the Write accessory). This command allows you to view representative samples of the screen fonts, as well as to add and remove fonts.

If you choose to add fonts, you will have the opportunity to select a font file to add. This will probably be a file provided by a third party. You should specify where the font resides, select the font file, and then click on OK. When you do, Windows adds the font to the available font list.

When you remove a font, it is not deleted from your hard drive. It is only removed from the list of fonts actively available to Windows. You may wish to remove fonts that you rarely or never use. Doing so will free some memory and hard disk space for other uses.

Tips

Keep in mind that working with fonts requires both memory and processing time. If you use a lot of fonts, chances are good that your overall processing time will be longer for any given task. On the other hand, judicious use of fonts can give your work a very attractive professional appearance.

Never remove the MS Sans Serif font, since it is used for window titles and dialog boxes.

FORMAT DISK

File Manager

The Format Disk command prepares a blank disk to receive files.

Menu Structure

Disk | Format Disk...

Steps

Keyboard: ALT-D-F
Mouse: Click on Disk menu, then click on Format Disk...

Notes

Before you can store information on a disk, it must be formatted. This command allows you to format a disk and optionally put system files on it. These system files are necessary if you want to make the disk bootable.

When you choose this command, you are given the opportunity to select which disk drive to use. (If you do not physically have a B drive, Windows assumes you will format using drive A.) Select a drive. You will then be able to indicate whether the disk is to be high capacity, and whether this is meant to be a system disk. Make your choices and select OK; the disk will be formatted.

Warning: Format Disk is a destructive command. It will erase any existing data on a disk. Be sure you really want to format a disk before you use this command.

Tips

If you have already formatted a disk, and you later decide you need to make it a system disk, you do not have to reformat it. Use the Make System Disk command; it is quicker and easier.

GLOSSARY

Help System

The Glossary button in the Help System allows you to view the definitions of command terms related to the help file.

Menu Structure

Steps

Keyboard: ALT-G
Mouse: Click on Glossary button

Notes

The Help System built into Windows is very
powerful. It displays information from a help file in
a consistent and clear manner. These help files
have the HLP file extension. If, when loading an
application program, Windows discovers that there
is a help file that has the same root filename as the
application program, that help file is opened and
ready for use.

The Help System is great at indicating what steps
need to happen when, in a general way. There are
times, however, when you may not fully understand
a term being used in the help file. This command
allows you to see an alphabetical list of terms, and
then view their definitions. You can also directly
view terms in the glossary by double-clicking on
any term that has a dotted underline.

This is an optional command. Its availability
depends on the help file being viewed. Some help
files have glossaries, while others don't.

HIGH PRIORITY

Print Manager

The High Priority command sets the priority level
for printing jobs handled by the Print Manager.

Menu Structure

Options | High Priority

Steps

Keyboard: ALT-O-H
Mouse: Click on Options menu, then click on
            High Priority

Notes

The Print Manager governs how Windows interacts
with your printer. It is a spooling utility, and its use
is completely optional. Since printers are usually
slower than computers, a spooling utility (such as
the Print Manager) allows information to be sent to
your printer at the speed your printer can accept it,
freeing up your computer to work on other tasks.

This is a toggle command, meaning the command
can be turned on and off. When you select the
command the first time, the priority level for what
the Print Manager does is set at its highest level,
and a check mark appears beside the command on
the menu. If you use another priority command
(Low Priority or Medium Priority), the check mark
moves to the other priority level.

This command controls what relative percentage of your computer's time is spent processing printing jobs. When set to high priority, then the work done by the Print Manager takes the largest percentage of your computer's time, even when there are other tasks running. It also means that your other tasks take longer to complete than if you used a lower priority setting for the Print Manager.

This command only affects system operation if there are print jobs waiting to print.

Tips

If you find that your other tasks are of greater importance than what you are printing out, use a lower priority setting for the Print Manager.

If you find that it is imperative that your other tasks not be interrupted by what the Print Manager is doing, pause output to the printers by selecting the printer and clicking on the Pause button.

HISTORY

Help System

The History button in the Help System allows you to select a previously viewed help screen.

Menu Structure

History

Steps

Keyboard: Aʟᴛ-T
Mouse: Click on History button

Notes

The Help System built into Windows is very
powerful. It displays information from a help file in
a consistent and clear manner. These help files
have the HLP file extension. If, when loading an
application program, Windows discovers that there
is a help file that has the same root filename as the
application program, that help file is opened and
ready for use.

When you use the Help System, every display action
you take using hyperlinks to other help topics is
remembered by the system. Hyperlinks are active
links between the current Help topic and another
Help topic. Clicking on a highlighted hyperlink
displays the related help information about the
highlighted term or concept. The History command
button allows you to immediately jump to any
previously viewed screen.

Tips

If you only need to go back a few screens, you can
use the Back command. It steps you backward
through the History listing.

IGNORE IF INACTIVE

Print Manager

The Ignore if Inactive command turns off Print Manager error reporting when the Print Manager is inactive.

Menu Structure

Options | Ignore if Inactive

Steps

Keyboard: Alt-O-I
Mouse: Click on Options menu, then click on Ignore if Inactive

Notes

The Print Manager governs how Windows interacts with your printer. It is a spooling utility, and its use is completely optional. Since printers are usually slower than computers, a spooling utility (such as the Print Manager) allows information to be sent to your printer at the speed your printer can accept it, freeing up your computer to work on other tasks.

This is a toggle command, meaning the command can be turned on and off. When you select the command the first time, the error notification status for the Print Manager is changed, and a check mark appears beside the command on the menu. If you use another error notification command (Alert Always or Flash if Inactive), the check mark moves to the other command setting.

Typically the work done by the Print Manager is not done in an active window. It is usually done in the background while you are concentrating on other, more pressing tasks. Using this command determines how the Print Manager notifies you if it detects a condition that demands your attention.

After this command, if the Print Manager is in an inactive window or is minimized, any condition requiring your attention is ignored. If the Print Manager is the active window, however, the error message dialog box is displayed immediately.

Tips

It is best not to use this notification option. If you do, you run the risk of not getting some of your printed output because you were not able to correct a situation that required your intervention.

INDICATE EXPANDABLE BRANCHES

File Manager

The Indicate Expandable Branches command controls the display of icon information.

Menu Structure

Tree | Indicate Expandable Branches

Steps

Keyboard: Alt-T-I
Mouse: Click on Tree menu, then click on Indicate Expandable Branches

Notes

This is a toggle option, meaning the same command turns the option on and off. When you select the command the first time, a check mark appears beside the command on the menu. Select Indicate Expandable Branches again, and the check mark disappears.

When this option is enabled, the individual file folders in the directory tree (each of which represents a directory) are altered. If there are no subdirectories within a displayed directory, then the file folder is blank on the face. If there are subdirectorys, then the face of the file folder contains a plus sign. For commands affecting the display of the directory tree, see Collapse Branch, Expand All, Expand Branch, and Expand One Level.

INTERNATIONAL SETTINGS

Control Panel

The International Settings command allows you to change global values for language, keyboard, measurements, date, time, and numbers.

Menu Structure

International

Settings | International...

Steps

Keyboard: Aʟᴛ-S-I
Mouse: Click on Settings menu, then click on
             International...; or double-click on the
             International icon

Notes

Use of computers, and thus use of Windows, is not
limited to the United States. This command allows
you to change settings to customize Windows and
Windows applications for differing international
display standards.

You can change the following with this command:

Country   Allows you to select a desired country
from a list presented onscreen. When a country
is selected, default options are set for that
country. You can alter the individual settings for
that country, however, by changing any of the
other options listed in the rest of this section.

Language   The Language setting is used to
change the sorting and case conversion
procedures of some Windows applications.

Keyboard Layout   If you use an international
keyboard (one for a country other than the United
States), select the appropriate country from the
list. Your selection informs Windows how to
interpret what you type.

Measurement   The Measurement setting lets
you select English or Metric measurements.

List Separator   The List Separator setting
determines which character is used to

distinguish between elements in a list of words. Typically this is the comma, but it can be changed to any character you desire.

Date Format   The Date Format setting lets you choose how you want Windows to display dates.

Time Format   The Time Format setting lets you choose how you want Windows to display the time of day.

Currency Format   With the Currency Format setting, you specify the currency symbol (the dollar sign, the British pound sign, and so on) and its placement in relation to numbers, how negative numbers are represented, and how many decimal places to use.

Number Format   With the Number Format setting, you select which characters to use to separate thousands and to signify decimal values, as well as whether leading zeros are displayed.

Tips

Use of the International Settings command is not just for international users. You may wish to change settings because of a personal preference for how the time and date are displayed.

KEYBOARD SETTINGS

Control Panel

The Keyboard Settings command changes the repeat rate for the keyboard.

Menu Structure

Keyboard

Settings I Keyboard...

Steps

Keyboard: Aʟᴛ-S-K
Mouse: Click on Settings menu, then click on
                 Keyboard...; or double-click on the
                 Keyboard icon

Notes

The Keyboard Settings allow you to change how
long Windows should wait before beginning to
repeat a keypress and the rate at which keypresses
repeat. These are relative settings, on a scale of
slow to fast. You should select settings based on
your typing ability and preferences. The slower the
setting, the longer you will need to hold a key
before it repeats.

This command does not allow you to change the
type of keyboard you are using. You should see the
Change System Settings command for more
information on doing that.

LABEL DISK

File Manager

The Label Disk command allows you to set, change,
or delete a label assigned to a disk.

Menu Structure

Disk | Label Disk...

Steps

Keyboard: ALT-D-L
Mouse: Click on Disk menu, then click on Label
Disk...

Notes

Assigning a label to a disk is really nothing more
than naming the disk. This name can be up to 11
characters long and should follow the same naming
conventions used for naming disk files.

When you select this command, you will be shown
any existing disk label. If you want to delete an
existing disk label, simply press the BACKSPACE key
once right after selecting this command.

LOW PRIORITY

Print Manager

The Low Priority command sets the priority level for
printing jobs handled by the Print Manager.

Menu Structure

Options | Low Priority

Steps

Keyboard: Aʟᴛ-O-P
Mouse: Click on Options menu, then click on
Low Priority

Notes

The Print Manager governs how Windows interacts
with your printer. It is a spooling utility, and its use
is completely optional. Since printers are usually
slower than computers, a spooling utility (such as
the Print Manager) allows information to be sent to
your printer at the speed your printer can accept it,
freeing up your computer to work on other tasks.

This is a toggle command, meaning the command
can be turned on and off. When you select the
command the first time, the priority level for what
Print Manager does is set at the lowest level, and a
check mark appears beside the command on the
menu. If you use another priority command
(Medium Priority or High Priority), the check mark
moves to the other priority level.

The Low Priority command controls what relative
percentage of your computer's time is spent
processing printing jobs. When set to low priority,
then the work done by the Print Manager takes a
lesser percentage when your computer is busy
doing other tasks. It also means that your other
tasks receive a greater percentage of time, and
therefore complete faster.

This command only affects system operation if there
are print jobs waiting to print. Also, the throughput
of the Print Manager is affected by this command

only if there are other demands on your computer's
time (there are other active tasks running).

Tips

If you find that your print jobs are not completing
fast enough, or you are getting time-out errors on
your printer, select a higher priority setting for the
Print Manager.

MAKE SYSTEM DISK

File Manager

The Make System Disk command transfers system
files to a formatted disk.

Menu Structure

Disk | Make System Disk...

Steps

Keyboard: ALT-D-M
Mouse: Click on Disk menu, then click on Make
            System Disk...

Notes

If you want to make a disk bootable, you must first
transfer system files to it. The Make System Disk
command accomplishes that task with a previously
formatted disk.

In order for this command to work, you must have the current drive set to the one from which you normally boot your computer. For most people, this will be drive C. If you do not do this, Windows will not be able to locate the system files and will display an error message.

Under certain circumstances, Windows will not be able to complete this command. Generally this happens if the disk you want to make into a system disk already has files stored on it. You have the greatest chance of success when you use an empty disk for this operation.

Tips

If the disk is completely blank, or if you wish to permanently erase all the files on the disk, use the Format Disk command. Make sure you select the option to make the newly formatted disk a system disk.

MAXIMIZE WINDOW

System-wide

The Maximize Window command expands the current window to fill the entire screen.

Menu Structure

Control | Maximize

Steps

Keyboard: Alt–Dash–X for a document window,
        Alt–Spacebar–X for all other windows
Mouse: Click on the Control menu, then click on
        Maximize

Notes

The Control menu is accessed through the icon in
the upper-left corner of a window.

For readers who are not using a mouse, this is the
command provided to expand an icon to full screen,
or to expand an open window to fill the entire
screen. This command is only available if the
window has not already been maximized.

Tips

If you are using a mouse, simply click on the
upward-pointing arrow in the upper-right corner of
the screen. This does the same task as the
Maximize Window command.

MEDIUM PRIORITY

Print Manager

The Medium Priority command sets the priority
level for printing jobs handled by the Print Manager.

Menu Structure

Options | Medium Priority

Steps

Keyboard: Alt-O-M
Mouse: Click on Options menu, then click on
Medium Priority

Notes

The Print Manager governs how Windows interacts
with your printer. It is a spooling utility, and its use
is completely optional. Since printers are usually
slower than computers, a spooling utility (such as
the Print Manager) allows information to be sent to
your printer at the speed your printer can accept it,
freeing up your computer to work on other tasks.

This is a toggle command, meaning the command
can be turned on and off. When you select the
command the first time, the priority level for what
the Print Manager does is set at an intermediate
level, and a check mark appears beside the
command on the menu. If you use another priority
command (Low Priority or High Priority), the check
mark moves to the other priority level.

This command controls what relative percentage of
your computer's time is spent processing printing
jobs. When set to medium priority, the work done
by the Print Manager takes an intermediate
percentage when your computer is busy doing other
tasks. It also means that your other tasks take
longer to complete than if you used a low priority
setting for the Print Manager.

This command only affects system operation if there
are print jobs waiting to print. Also, the throughput
of the Print Manager is affected by this command

only if there are other demands on your computer's
time (there are other active tasks running).

Tips

If you find that your print jobs are not completing
fast enough, or you are getting time-out errors on
your printer, use the High Priority command to
select a higher priority level for the Print Manager.

If you find that your other tasks are of greater
importance than what you are printing out, use the
Low Priority command.

If you find that it is imperative that your other tasks
not be interrupted by what the Print Manager is
doing, pause output to the printers by selecting the
printer and clicking on the Pause button.

MINIMIZE ON USE

Program Manager or File Manager

The Minimize on Use command controls whether
the Program Manager or File Manager is
automatically minimized to a single icon when an
application is started.

Menu Structure

Options | Minimize on Use

Steps

Keyboard: Alt-O-M
Mouse: Click on Options menu, then click on
           Minimize on Use

Notes

This is a toggle option, meaning the same command
turns the option on and off. When you select the
command the first time, a check mark appears
beside the command on the menu. Select Minimize
on Use again, and the check mark disappears.

With Minimize on Use enabled, Windows
automatically shrinks, or *minimizes*, the window
when an application is run. For instance, if you are
using the File Manager and then start another
application without closing the File Manager first,
the File Manager is minimized to an icon. The
screen is then maximized for the application being
run.

When you exit the application program, you will
need to open the Program Manager or File Manager
icon again. The benefit of this command is that it
automatically causes maximum screen space to be
given to the application on which you're working.

The use of this command is a personal preference.
It does not affect the overall functioning of
Windows.

MINIMIZE WINDOW

System-wide

The Minimize Window command shrinks the current window to an icon.

Menu Structure

Control | Minimize

Steps

Keyboard: Alt–Dash–N for a document window,
Alt–Spacebar–N for all other windows
Mouse: Click on the Control menu, then click on Minimize

Notes

The Control menu is accessed through the icon in the upper-left corner of a window.

For readers who are not using a mouse, this is the command provided to shrink a window to a single icon. This command is only available if the window has not already been minimized.

Tips

If you are using a mouse, simply click on the downward-pointing arrow in the upper-right corner of the screen. This does the same task as the Minimize Window command.

MOUSE SETTINGS

Control Panel

The Mouse Settings command lets you change how your mouse functions in relation to Windows.

Menu Structure

Mouse

Settings | Mouse...

Steps

Keyboard: Alt-S-M
Mouse: Click on Settings menu, then click on Mouse...; or double-click on the Mouse icon

Notes

If you are like most Windows users, your mouse is integral to productive use of Windows. This command allows you to change several settings that affect how Windows reacts to your mouse. These settings are

Mouse Tracking Speed   The Mouse Tracking Speed setting controls how fast the mouse curser onscreen moves when you move the mouse. This is a relative setting, from slow to fast; the slower the setting, the slower the mouse cursor moves.

Double Click Speed   The Double Click Speed
setting controls the amount of time allowed
between mouse clicks before the two clicks can
be considered one double-click. This is a relative
setting, from slow to fast; the slower the setting,
the more time allowed between successive clicks.

Swap Left/Right Buttons   Toggle the Swap Left/
Right Buttons setting if you wish the actions
caused by the left and right mouse buttons to be
reversed.

Mouse Trails   When this option is selected, the
mouse leaves a trail as it moves across the
screen. This is helpful for LCD screens on which
the mouse might normally be hard to locate.

MOVE

Program Manager

The Move command allows you to move a program
from one program group to another.

Menu Structure

File | Move...

Steps

Keyboard: Alt-F-M
Shortcut: F7
Mouse: Click on File menu, then click on Move...

Notes

For readers who are not using a mouse, the Move command is what you use to move program icons from one program group to another. Select the icon you wish to move, and then issue this command. You will be prompted for the name of the group to which you want the program moved.

Tips

If you are using a mouse, you can accomplish this task much more easily. All you need to do is click on the program icon and drag it to the program group where you want it to be.

Use the Copy Program Item command if you want to duplicate an icon into another program group.

MOVE FILE

File Manager

The Move File command moves files or directories from one place to another.

Menu Structure

File | Move...

Steps

Keyboard: Alt-F-M
Shortcut: F7
Mouse: Click on File menu, then click on Move...

Notes

The Move File command allows you to move files or
entire subdirectories from one place to another. If
the place you are moving from (the *source*) and the
place you are moving to (the *destination*) are both
on the same disk, and you are using a mouse, you
simply need to drag the icon for the file or directory
to the destination. If desired, the destination can be
the icon for another drive.

If you are not using a mouse, you should select the
Move File command. You can then specify the *from*
and *to* locations for the move, using wildcard
characters to move multiple files in one operation.
The source and destination do not need to be on the
same drive.

Basically, Move File copies the designated files or
subdirectories to the new location and then deletes
them from their original location.

Tips

If you are using a mouse and the source and
destination are on different drives, you can open
multiple windows for the directories on the differing
drives. Then simply hold down the SHIFT key and
drag the files or subdirectories between windows.

MOVE WINDOW

System-wide

The Move Window command allows you to move a
window around the screen.

Menu Structure

Control | Move

Steps

Keyboard: ALT-DASH-M for a document window,
ALT-SPACEBAR-M for all other windows
Mouse: Click on the Control menu, then click on
Move

Notes

The Control menu is accessed through the icon in
the upper-left corner of a window.

For readers not using a mouse, the Move Window
command is what you use to move individual
windows around the desktop. When you select this
command, a positioning cursor will appear on the
screen. You can then use the arrow keys to move
the window. When you are satisfied with the new
window position, press ENTER to accept the new
position, or ESC to cancel the move.

The use of this command is personal preference.
There is no real benefit to where windows are
located on the screen, other than to make your work
easier.

Tips

If you have a mouse, simply click on the window's
title bar and drag it to any position on the screen.

NETWORK CONNECTIONS

File Manager

The Network Connections command controls the mapping of network directories to individual drives.

Menu Structure

Disk | Network Connections...

Steps

Keyboard: Alt-D-N
Mouse: Click on Disk menu, then click on
            Network Connections...

Notes

This command is only available if your computer is connected to a network. Depending on your network software, you are able to assign logical areas of the network drives to drive letters which you can use. For instance, a directory on the file server could be assigned to drive N:, or a volume on a different file server could be assigned to drive R:.

The Network Connections command allows you to control this mapping. If any previous mapping has been done, the currently mapped drives are displayed.

NETWORK CONNECTIONS

Print Manager

The Network Connections command controls
selection of network printers.

Menu Structure

Options I Network Connections...

Steps

Keyboard: Alt-O-C
Mouse: Click on Options menu, then click on
            Network Connections...

Notes

If your computer is connected to a network, there is
a good chance you have access to network printers.
This command allows you to define which printers
the Print Manager should access when printing
information. Once you have selected printers, you
can use the Network Settings command to control
how the Print Manager works with the network.

NETWORK SETTINGS

Control Panel

The Network Settings command provides a way to
access network utilities.

Menu Structure

Network
Settings | Network...

Steps

Keyboard: ALT-S-N
Mouse: Click on Settings menu, then click on
Network...; or double-click on the
Network icon

Notes

This command is available only if your computer is
attached to a network. It provides a way for you to
access basic network utilities. When you choose
this command, you are presented with a dialog box
that indicates the type of network you are attached
to, and asked what network utility you want to run.

You can run any network utility; a few of them are
built into the network driver you installed with
Windows. Exactly what options are available
depends on your network. For instance, if you are
using Novell NetWare, the built-in utilities are:

Attach a File Server
Detach a File Server
Disable Broadcast Messages
Enable Broadcast Messages

Tips

Make sure the communications settings used in
Windows match the communications parameters

expected by the external device. If they don't, you won't be able to establish a working connection.

NETWORK SETTINGS

Print Manager

The Network Settings command controls how the Print Manager works with a network.

Menu Structure

Options | Network Settings...

Steps

Keyboard: Aʟᴛ-O-N
Mouse: Click on Options menu, then click on Network Settings...

Notes

This command allows you to control how Windows sends information to a network printer. If desired, you can choose for Windows to print directly to a network queue, thereby disabling the Print Manager. This generally results in faster network printing, and the Print Manager will remain active only to relay network queue status reports.

This command also controls whether the Print Manager updates the network queue display periodically.

NEW

Program Manager

The New command lets you designate a new program or create a new program group.

Menu Structure

File | New...

Steps

Keyboard: ALT-F-N
Mouse: Click on File menu, then click on New...

Notes

This command is most-often used to add program groups to the Program Manager, but can also be used to add application programs within program groups.

When you choose this command you are asked to specify whether you are setting up a program group or a *program item*. A program item is represented in the Program Manager as an icon, and is used to start an application program. Make your choice and press ENTER.

If you are adding a program group, you are asked for the description and group filename. The description is the name that appears under the icon or in the title bar when the program group is opened as a window. The group filename is the DOS file used by Windows to track what is included in this program group. You do not need to provide a group filename_Windows will create one automatically.

If you are adding a program item, you are asked for the description and the command line to be executed when the icon is selected. The description is the name that appears under the icon on the desktop, as well as in the title bar of the window when the application is running. The command line is the DOS command executed when the icon is selected, or started. This command line consists of the full path name to the program file, including the disk drive (if necessary). When you supply these items and press ENTER, Windows will create an appropriate icon for the type of program you added.

If you want to change either a program group or a program item, use the Properties command.

Tips

For frequently used programs, you can have program groups created automatically by the Set Up Applications command.

If you are adding a program group and you do not designate a filename, Windows will use the first eight legal characters of the description as a root filename, along with the extension GRP. If you have multiple groups where the first eight characters of the description are the same, you must provide a unique program group filename when creating the program group.

NEW WINDOW

File Manager

The New Window command creates a new directory window.

Menu Structure

Window | New Window

Steps

Keyboard: Aʟᴛ-W-N
Mouse: Click on Window menu, then click on
            New Window

Notes

Many times it is helpful to look at more than one directory at a time. This command allows you to create additional directory windows. Each window has the same display characteristics as the current window. Once they are created, however, windows can be individually tailored to display directories in different manners.

Tips

You can also create a new directory window by double-clicking on a drive icon.

NEXT WINDOW

System-wide

The Next Window command makes the next document window the active window.

Menu Structure

Control | Next

Steps

Keyboard: ALT-DASH-T
Shortcut: CTRL-F6
Mouse: Click on the Control menu, then click on Next

Notes

The Control menu is accessed through the icon in the upper-left corner of a window.

This command is only available if there are multiple document windows open on your screen. This command causes Windows to cycle through each of them, one after the other. It is mainly provided for users without a mouse, or is useful to access windows completely hidden by other windows.

Tips

If you are using a mouse, and you can see any portion of the desired window, click on that portion to access the window. This is much faster than using the Next Window command.

OPEN

Program Manager or File Manager

The Open command lets you open a subdirectory or a file, or start a program.

Menu Structure

File | Open

Steps

Keyboard: ALT-F-O
Shortcut: ENTER
Mouse: Click on File menu, then click on Open

Notes

Within the Program Manager, the Open command is used to start applications. When you issue the Open command, Windows will attempt to load and run the currently selected application.

Within the File Manager, this command is generally used to open directories, although it can be used to open documents that are associated with programs. If you try to open a file that has no program association, you will get an error message. If you use this command to open an application program or PIF file, Windows will attempt to run the application or the program associated with the PIF file. For more information on associated files, see the Associate File command.

When you use this command to open a directory in the File Manager, it has the same effect as double-clicking on the directory icon.

Tips

You can also open directories or files by double-clicking on their icon.

OPEN CLIPBOARD FILE

Clipboard

The Open Clipboard File command opens and loads a previously saved Clipboard.

Menu Structure

File | Open...

Steps

Keyboard: Alt-F-O
Mouse: Click on File menu, then click on Open...

Notes

This command allows you to open Clipboard files created by the Save As command. Clipboard files have the extension CLP. The information in these files can be text or graphics; indeed, it can be any data that might be exchanged between applications via the Clipboard.

Information is put into and taken out of the Clipboard with editing commands, the most common of which are Copy, Cut, and Paste.

When you choose the Open Clipboard File command, you are prompted for a filename. You are shown a series of files with the CLP extension. You may choose one of those or directly enter a filename to be opened.

Also see the Save As command.

Tips

If you find yourself pasting the same graphic (such as a logo or special symbol) again and again, copy it into the Clipboard and save it to disk. Then you can access the file at a later date and paste it into whatever you are working on at the time.

If you use this command while there is data in the Clipboard, the old data will be cleared before the new file is loaded. If the Clipboard currently contains information you want to save, do so before using the Open Clipboard File command.

OPEN FILE

Help System

The Open File command opens a specific Help System file.

Menu Structure

File | Open...

Steps

Keyboard: Alt-F-O
Mouse: Click on File menu, then click on Open...

Notes

The information displayed by the Windows Help System is contained in a series of help files. When you enter the Help System, Windows displays the help file that it deems most appropriate to the context of what you are doing. This command allows you to open a different help file from the one Windows would show you.

Help files have the file extension HLP. When you choose the Open File command, you are shown a list of all the help files available in the current directory. You can navigate to another drive or directory to search for more help files, if desired. When you have found the help file you want to use, select it and click on the Open button. The help file is loaded and displayed.

Tips

Use this command if you want to refer to help for a particular program, but don't want to go through the hassle of loading the program and then accessing the Help System.

OTHER NET QUEUE

Print Manager

The Other Net Queue command lets you view the status of network printer queues to which you are not currently connected.

Menu Structure

View | Other Net Queue...

Steps

Keyboard: ALT-V-O
Mouse: Click on View menu, then click on Other Net Queue...

Notes

The Other Net Queue command is available only if you are connected to a network and using printing facilities for that network.

This command allows you to view the print jobs waiting in other network print queues besides the ones you are connected to. In this way, you can determine if you want to print to one of the other queues. If you do, you will still need to connect to that queue using the Printer Settings command from the Control Panel.

A network print queue is different than the print queue maintained by the Print Manager. The Print Manager maintains a queue of print jobs for your

computer alone. A network print queue is for the
print jobs of all users attached to the network.

PORT SETTINGS

Control Panel

The Port Settings command lets you set parameters
for serial communications ports.

Menu Structure

Ports

Settings ⏐ Ports...

Steps

Keyboard: Aʟᴛ-S-O
Mouse: Click on Settings menu, then click on
            Ports...; or double-click on the Ports icon

Notes

Your computer typically has two serial ports, and
can have as many as four. Each port has
parameters that control how communications with
external devices occur.

The Port Settings command allows you to change
the communications parameters for the four
communications (COM) ports. For each port you
can change the baud rate (110 bps to 19.2 Kbps), the
number of data bits, the parity, the number of stop
bits, and the type of flow control used.

Tips

Make sure the communications settings used in Windows match the communications parameters expected by the external device. If they don't, you won't be able to establish a working connection.

Setting port parameters with this command indicates to Windows how it should expect to communicate with a serial printer attached to a specific communications port. If you use other programs that also use the serial ports (such as the Cardfile and Terminal accessories), use those programs to set communications settings as well.

PRINT FILE

File Manager

The Print File command sends a text file to the default printer.

Menu Structure

File | Print...

Steps

Keyboard: Alt-F-P
Mouse: Click on File menu, then click on Print...

Notes

The Print File command allows you to print a file without having to start the application used to create it. This command is very minimalistic_it simply copies the file to the printer. There is no special formatting or handling done with the file. Thus, this command is only useful for straight text files (ASCII files). If the file is not a text file, or if you want to include special formatting, you will need to use another application program.

When you choose this command, you are asked to specify the file you want to print. The default is the file selected in the active directory window. If you want to select a different file, you enter the filename here. After entering the filename, the File Manager sends the specified file to the default printer. If you need to change the printer, see the Print Setup command.

Tips

Do not use this command for printing formatted word processing documents. The output from your printer is likely to be gibberish.

PRINT SETUP

Help System

The Print Setup command lets you select and set up printers from within the Help System.

Menu Structure

File | Print Setup...

Steps

Keyboard: ALT-F-R
Mouse: Click on File menu, then click on Print
                 Setup...

Notes

While the primary method of setting up printers is
done through the Control Panel command Printer
Settings, the Print Setup command in the Help
System allows you to select an available printer and
optionally set it up.

When you select this command, you are shown a list
of printers that Windows believes is connected to
your system. If the list is incorrect, or if the port
assignments for any of the printers is incorrect, you
will need to use the Print Setup command to change
them. If the printer you want to use from within the
Help System is shown in the list, select it. Then you
can click on the Setup button to change specific
options that control the printer you have selected.

Because there are literally hundreds of setup
options for the dozens of printers that could be
connected to Windows, detailed coverage of printer
setup options is beyond the scope of this pocket
reference. For further information, see *Windows
3.1: The Complete Reference* by Tom Sheldon.

Tips

If you have only one printer connected to your
system and you have already set it up using Printer
Settings, you don't need to use the Print Setup
command. Printer settings remain constant across
applications unless you explicitly change them.

PRINT TOPIC

Help System

The Print Topic command copies a major Help System section to the printer.

Menu Structure

File | Print Topic

Steps

Keyboard: Aʟт-F-P
Mouse: Click on File menu, then click on Print
            Topic

Notes

The Print Topic command copies a Help System section to your printer. Make sure you have selected and set up the desired printer, either with the Printer Settings command (available from the Control Panel) or with the Print Setup command (from within the Help System).

PRINTER SETTINGS

Control Panel

The Printer Settings command allows you to select and configure printers connected to your system.

Menu Structure

Printers   Settings | Printers...

Steps

Keyboard: Alt-S-P
Mouse: Click on Settings menu, then click on
            Printers...; or double-click on the Printers
            icon

Notes

Besides data communications, printers tend to be
one of the most complicated areas of computing.
When you installed Windows, you had the
opportunity to specify what printers you had and
how they were connected to your computer. After
Windows has been installed, the Printer Settings
command allows you to select a printer (if you have
more than one) and configure it. If you want to add
another printer to your system, you can also do that
with this command.

When you select the Printer Settings command, you
are presented with a list of printers that Windows
believes are connected to your computer. The
heading at the top of this list says "Installed
Printers." The highlighted printer is the one
currently designated to receive output from your
system.

If you click on the Connect button, you can set port
specifications for the selected printer. You can
specify where each printer is to be connected.

These connections can be any of three parallel ports, four serial ports, an EPT port, or a file. This port setting determines the destination of the information that Windows prints. If you choose a serial port, then you should see the information under the Port Settings command to be sure your communications settings are properly set.

If you click on the Setup button, you can further define how Windows should treat the printer you have selected. Here you can select printer-specific settings that determine how Windows will control the printer. Because there are literally hundreds of setup options for the dozens of printers that could be connected to Windows, detailed coverage of printer setup options is beyond the scope of this pocket reference. For further information in this area, see *Windows 3.1: The Complete Reference* by Tom Sheldon.

Another important function of this command is that you can specify whether the Print Manager should be used with your printer. This is the portion of Windows that controls the orderly printing of files to your printer.

Tips

You can print a Windows document for a printer you don't have connected to your system by directing output to a file. When you attempt to print, you will be asked for a filename. Supply one, and Windows will send information to the file instead of to a printer. However, the information in the file will still be formatted for the target printer.

For instance, you might not have a PostScript printer attached to your computer, but you wish to

produce some PostScript output. When you have
printed the document to the file, you can do the
following:

1. Copy the file to a disk.
2. Take the disk to a computer that has a
    PostScript printer attached.
3. Using the DOS copy command (or the
    Windows Copy File command), copy the file to
    the port to which the printer is connected.

The result is that you will be able to print your
document as if the PostScript printer was connected
to your system.

PRINTER SETUP

Print Manager

The Printer Setup command allows you to configure
a printer.

Menu Structure

Options | Printer Setup...

Steps

Keyboard: Alt-O-P
Mouse: Click on Options menu, then click on
Printer Setup...

Notes

This command performs a function similar to that done by the Printer Settings command. With it, you can change the setup of a specific printer attached to your computer. Here you can select printer-specific settings that determine how Windows will control the printer. Because there are literally hundreds of setup options for the dozens of printers that could be connected to Windows, detailed coverage of printer setup options is beyond the scope of this pocket reference. For further information in this area, see *Windows 3.1: The Complete Reference* by Tom Sheldon.

PROPERTIES

File Manager

The Properties command changes the attributes assigned to a file.

Menu Structure

File | Properties...

Steps

Keyboard: Alt-F-T
Shortcut: Alt-Enter
Mouse: Click on File menu, then click on Properties...

Notes

Within the DOS environment (and therefore within Windows), files can possess attributes, or *properties*, that define how they are treated by the operating system. There are four properties that can be modified by this command. They are

Read-only   If the read-only attribute is enabled, the file cannot be deleted or changed. It can only be read by a program.

Archive   If the archive attribute is enabled, it means that the file has been changed since it was last backed up.

Hidden   If the hidden attribute is enabled, it means that the file will not appear in normal directory listings_it is hidden from view.

System   If the system attribute is enabled, it means the file is designated as a file to be used by the operating system (DOS). System files are not normally displayed in directory listings.

You can still view system and hidden files by telling Windows to display them. This is done using the View By File Type command in the File Manager.

If you change a directory's properties so that it is hidden, the directory tree display will only be affected when the directory is read from disk again. This typically occurs when you add or delete a directory or when you expand or collapse branches.

PROPERTIES

Program Manager

The Properties command changes how Windows displays a program group or an application program.

Menu Structure

File | Properties...

Steps

Keyboard: ALT-F-P
Shortcut: ALT-ENTER
Mouse: Click on File menu, then click on Properties...

Notes

When you are ready to use the Properties command, be sure you have first selected the program group or application program whose properties you wish to modify.

If you are changing the properties of an application program (called a *program item*), then you can change the description, command line to be executed, and the icon. The description is the name that appears under the icon on the desktop, as well as in the title bar of the window when the application is running. The command line is the DOS command Windows executes when the icon is opened. The icon is the graphic representation of the application program.

If you minimize a program group window, select it, and then choose this command, you are given the opportunity to change the properties assigned to the whole program group. These properties consist of the description and the group file designation. The description is the name that appears under the icon and at the top of the group window. The group filename is the DOS file used to define what is included in this program group.

For more information, see the New command.

REFRESH

File Manager

The Refresh command forces an update of the directory windows in the File Manager.

Menu Structure

Window | Refresh

Steps

Keyboard: Alt-W-R
Shortcut: F5
Mouse: Click on Window menu, then click on Refresh

Notes

The File Manager generally does a pretty good job of reflecting file changes and automatically updating after every operation. However, if you have several programs working simultaneously or you are working in a networked environment, it is possible for some File Manager windows to not be updated. If you suspect this has happened, use the Refresh command. It forces a refresh of the information displayed in the windows.

Tips

If you are connected to a network, and your computer has been idle for a while, issue the Refresh command. That way you will be sure you are seeing the current state of affairs.

REFRESH

Print Manager

The Refresh command forces an update of the files in a network print queue.

Menu Structure

View | Refresh

Steps

Keyboard: Alt-V-R
Shortcut: F5
Mouse: Click on View menu, then click on Refresh

Notes

When you are printing to a network queue, the Print Manager periodically updates the status of the queue. However, you may want information right away, without waiting on the Print Manager. This command forces an update of the queue information immediately.

RENAME

File Manager

The Rename command allows you to rename a file or subdirectory.

Menu Structure

File | Rename...

Steps

Keyboard: ALT-F-N
Mouse: Click on File menu, then click on Rename...

Notes

This command is used to change the name of either a file or subdirectory. When you choose the command, you are shown the old name for the item and asked to enter a new name. The currently selected item is shown as a default for the old name. If the old name is incorrect, you can move the text cursor and change it.

Once you have verified the old name and provided a new name, click on the Rename button. The change will be completed.

If a file has the read-only property enabled, it cannot be renamed without first disabling the property. For more information, see the Properties command.

RESTORE WINDOW

System-wide

The Restore Window command restores the current window to its normal size.

Menu Structure

Control | Restore

Steps

Keyboard: ALT-DASH-R for a document window, ALT-SPACEBAR-R for all other windows

Mouse: Click on the Control menu, then click on Restore

Notes

The Control menu is accessed through the icon in the upper-left corner of a window.

For readers who are not using a mouse, this is the command provided to restore a window to an "in-between" size_it is neither minimized nor maximized. It is the size created with your last sizing operation. The resulting window can be resized using the Size Window command. This command is only available if the window has either been minimized or maximized.

Tips

If you are using a mouse and the window is maximized, simply click on the icon containing both an upward- and downward-pointing arrow. This icon is near the upper-right corner of the window.

If you are using a mouse, and the window is minimized, simply double-click on the icon to restore.

RUN

Program Manager or File Manager

The Run command allows you to run an application program.

Menu Structure

File | Run...

Steps

Keyboard: Alt-F-R
Mouse: Click on File menu, then click on Run...

Notes

This is one method used to run programs within Windows. When you choose this command, you are asked to enter a command line. This is the name of the program you want to run, followed by any parameters that the program may require. When you press ENTER, Windows will attempt to load and execute the program.

If you check the box that says "Run Minimized," then the program is started and automatically minimized. It will then appear as an icon at the bottom of your desktop.

The Run command is the same as using the Open command with the program icon selected.

Tips

If you are using a mouse, there are two additional ways you can start a program. First, you can double-click on the icon for the program. This is a fast, efficient way to begin a program that has been set up for use with Windows. If you are in the File Manager, you can also double-click on a PIF, EXE, or COM file to begin an application.

Second, if you are in the File Manager you can drag the icon for a data file on top of the icon for the program that will use the data file. Windows will attempt to load the program and the data file.

SAVE AS

Clipboard

The Save As command saves the contents of the Clipboard to a disk file.

Menu Structure

File | Save As...

Steps

Keyboard: Alt-F-A
Mouse: Click on File menu, then click on Save As...

Notes

The Save As command allows you to save whatever is in the Clipboard to a special Clipboard disk file. Clipboard files are saved with the extension CLP. When you choose this command you are prompted for a filename. You only need to enter up to eight characters for a filename; the CLP file extension is added automatically.

Anything that can be stored in the Clipboard can be saved with this command. Information is put into and taken out of the Clipboard with editing commands, the most common of which are Copy, Cut, and Paste.

The Clipboard is not cleared at the end of this command. If you want to clear the Clipboard to free up memory, you should use the Delete Clipboard command.

Also see the Open Clipboard File command.

Tips

If you find yourself pasting the same graphic (such as a logo or special symbol) again and again, copy it into the Clipboard and save it to disk. Then you can access the file at a later date and paste it into whatever you are working on at the time.

You can copy an entire Windows screen into the Clipboard simply by pressing the PRINTSCREEN key. You can then save the file to disk or paste it into a graphics program.

You can copy the active window into the Clipboard by pressing ALT-PRINTSCREEN.

It is a good idea to devise Clipboard filenames that indicate what is in the file. For instance, you might want graphics files to end in the characters GR. The code you devise is up to you.

SAVE SETTINGS ON EXIT

Program Manager or File Manager

The Save Settings on Exit command causes Windows to save the current environment settings until the next session.

Menu Structure

Options | Save Settings on Exit

Steps

Keyboard: ALT-O-E
Mouse: Click on Options menu, then click on
           Save Settings on Exit

Notes

This is a toggle option, meaning the same command turns the option on and off. When you select the command the first time, a check mark appears

beside the command on the menu, and Windows
will save environment settings when exiting. Select
Save Settings on Exit again, and the check mark
disappears and the feature is disabled.

The environment settings saved include display
settings and default program choices; it does not
include opening programs that were left open when
the File Manager or Program Manager was exited.

SEARCH

Help System

The Search button in the Help System allows you to
search for specific information among the topics
available in the current Help System file.

Menu Structure

Search

Steps

Keyboard: Aʟᴛ-S
Mouse: Click on Search button

Notes

The Help System built into Windows is very
powerful. It displays information from a help file in
a consistent and clear manner. These help files
have the HLP file extension. If, when you access
the Help System, Windows discovers that there is a
help file that has the same root filename as the

application program that is currently active, that help file is opened and ready for use.

Whoever designed the help file currently being used also decided what the major keywords were in the help file. These keywords are directly accessible with the Search command.

When you select this command, the following window will appear:

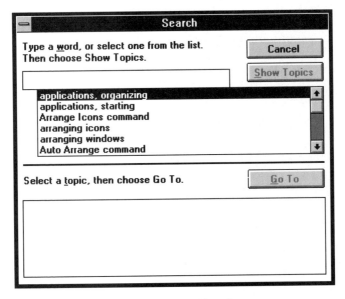

From this screen you can specify what you are searching for. The word you enter is called a *keyword*. As you type the keyword, the alphabetical list of keywords displayed under where you are typing will be updated so that the first letters of the top keyword shown matches the first letters of what you have typed. This means you don't have to type the whole word. You just have to type enough to be able to distinguish your keyword from all the other keywords available for the current help file.

When you click on the Search button or press Enter, you will be shown a list of the topics that include the keyword you entered. Then you can jump directly to any of the sections you desire. You can either highlight the topic and click on the Go To button, or you can double-click on the topic desired.

Tips

If you are unfamiliar with the subject matter and don't know the proper keyword to enter, you can browse through the available keywords by using the scroll bar to the right of the alphabetical keyword list.

SEARCH FOR FILES

File Manager

The Search for Files command lets you search for a specific file in either the current directory or over an entire disk.

Menu Structure

File I Search...

Steps

Keyboard: Alt-F-H
Mouse: Click on File menu, then click on Search...

Notes

When you choose this command, you are asked to provide a file specification for which to search. You can specify partial names or get really fancy with this parameter. Full discussion of filenames and wildcard characters is beyond the scope of this pocket reference. For more information, see *Simply DOS* or *DOS: The Complete Reference*, Third Edition, both by Kris Jamsa and published by Osborne/McGraw-Hill.

When you specify a filename template, the File Manager begins searching for files that match. When the search is complete, a window called Search Results is created, and all the located files are listed in it. If you directed the search to occur on the entire disk, then full path names are shown for the files.

Using the Search Results window, you can act on these files as if they were in a single directory. This allows for some very powerful operations to occur. For instance, if you have Excel spreadsheet files in various places all over your hard drive, you could search for all files ending in XLS. The File Manager will list all these files as a result of the search. Then you could move all these files to a single directory, or to another drive. The result is a quick and easy way to clean up your hard drive.

SELECT DRIVE

File Manager

The Select Drive command allows you to specify which drive should be displayed in the current directory window.

Menu Structure

Disk | Select Drive...

Steps

Keyboard: ALT-D-S
Mouse: Click on Disk menu, then click on Select Drive...

Notes

This command is used to change the drive which is displayed in the directory window. You are presented with a list of available drives, and all you need to do is select one. If you select a floppy drive, make sure there is a disk in the drive.

If you are using a mouse, it is much easier to simply click on the desired drive icon, or you can hold down the CTRL key and press the drive letter for the desired drive.

SELECT FILES

File Manager

The Select Files command lets you select a set of files within the current directory window.

Menu Structure

File | Select Files...

Steps

Keyboard: Alt-F-S
Mouse: Click on File menu, then click on Select
               Files...

Notes

The Select Files command is a powerful command that lets you build a selection set of files from the current directory. You start with no files selected, and then provide a filename to add to the selection set. You can use wildcard characters if you desire. Using the file specifications along with the Select and Deselect buttons, you can compile a set of files on which you wish to perform a subsequent action. This command is generally used in preparation for some other operation such as copying, moving, or deleting.

SELECTED NET QUEUE

Print Manager

The Selected Net Queue displays the queue status for a network print queue.

Menu Structure

View | Selected Net Queue...

Steps

Keyboard: ALT-V-S
Mouse: Click on View menu, then click on Selected Net Queue...

Notes

The Selected Net Queue command is available only if you are connected to a network and using printing facilities for that network. Also, you will only be able to use this command for network printers you are connected to. You connect to network printers by using the Printer Settings command from the Control Panel.

If the currently selected printer happens to be a network print queue, this command allows you to view a list of the print jobs waiting in the queue. This lets you see how your print jobs are progressing.

A network print queue is different than the print queue maintained by the Print Manager. The Print Manager maintains a queue of print jobs for your computer alone. A network print queue is for the print jobs of all users attached to the network.

SET UP APPLICATIONS

Windows Setup

The Set Up Applications command automatically adds program icons to Windows for your applications.

Menu Structure

Options | Set Up Applications...

Steps

Keyboard: Alt-O-S
Mouse: Click on Options menu, then click on Set
            Up Applications...

Notes

When you first installed Windows, you were given the option of having the installation program search through your hard drives to find application programs to install in Windows. The Set Up Applications command does the same thing. It allows you to search through any drive for applications that Windows recognizes and can install automatically.

If you did this when you installed Windows, you should only have to do it again if you make significant changes to the programs on your system. When you choose this command, you are asked to specify which drive or drives should be searched. Once this is done, the Windows Setup program searches the drives for programs it may recognize. You will then have the option of adding those programs to the system.

If you add a program, Windows will create an icon for it and add it to the Program Manager. If you choose to add a program that has previously been added, you will have two identical icons in the Program Manager that do the same thing. To remove one you will need to use the Delete command from the Program Manager.

SIZE WINDOW

System-wide

The Size Window command restores the current window to its normal size.

Menu Structure

Control | Size

Steps

Keyboard: ALT-DASH-S for a document window,
ALT-SPACEBAR-S for all other windows
Mouse: Click on the Control menu, then click on Size

Notes

The Control menu is accessed through the icon in the upper-left corner of a window.

If you are not using a mouse, this is the command provided to change the size of a window. When you choose the command, a multitipped arrow pointing in four directions appears. Press any of the following cursor-control keys for the desired action:

Left Arrow   The left arrow moves the left border of the window. The others stay in place.

Right Arrow   The right arrow moves the right border of the window. The others stay in place.

Up Arrow   The up arrow moves the top border of the window. The others stay in place.

Down Arrow   The down arrow moves the bottom border of the window. The others stay in place.

If you want to move a corner of the window, press two arrow keys simultaneously. For instance, if you want to move the window's lower-right corner, press the right and down arrows at the same time.

Once you have selected the border you want to move, use the arrow keys to move it in the direction desired. When you are satisfied with the move, press the ENTER key. If you press Esc, the sizing will be canceled.

The Size Window command is not available if the window has been minimized.

Tips

If you are using a mouse, click along any border of the window, or at any corner, and drag the border to the new position desired. This performs the same task as the Size Window command.

SORT BY DATE

File Manager

The Sort by Date command directs the File Manager to display files within the current directory window sorted by last modification date.

Menu Structure

View | Sort by Date

Steps

Keyboard: ALT-V-D
Mouse: Click on View menu, then click on Sort by Date

Notes

This is a toggle command, meaning the command can be turned on and off. When you select the command, a check mark appears beside the command on the menu. Select a different sorting option, and the check mark disappears.

When Sort by Date is selected, the File Manager sorts the directory display by the last modification date of the file, in descending order. This means that the most recently changed dates appear first. The modification date is either the date the file was created, or the date it was last written to. If two files were modified on the same date, then they are sorted by the last modification time, in descending order.

The usefulness of this command is questionable unless you also modify what the File Manager displays about each file. For full effect, you should either use the View All File Details command, or select to view the last modification date and time with the View Partial Details command.

For other sorting methods, see the Sort by Name, Sort by Size, and Sort by Type commands.

SORT BY NAME

File Manager

The Sort by Name command directs the File Manager to display files sorted by their names within the current directory window.

Menu Structure

View | Sort by Name

Steps

Keyboard: Alt-V-S
Mouse: Click on View menu, then click on Sort by Name

Notes

This is a toggle command, meaning the command can be turned on and off. When you select the command, a check mark appears beside the command on the menu. Select a different sorting option, and the check mark disappears.

When Sort by Name is selected, the File Manager sorts the files in the current directory window alphabetically by name. This is the normal sorting order for the File Manager. For other sorting methods, see the Sort by Date, Sort by Size, and Sort by Type commands.

SORT BY SIZE

File Manager

The Sort by Size command directs the File Manager to display files within the current directory window sorted by file size.

Menu Structure

View | Sort by Size

Steps

Keyboard: ALT-V-Z
Mouse: Click on View menu, then click on Sort by Size

Notes

This is a toggle command, meaning the command can be turned on and off. When you select the command, a check mark appears beside the command on the menu. Select a different sorting option, and the check mark disappears.

When Sort by Size is selected, the File Manager sorts the directory display by the size of each file, in bytes, in descending order.

The usefulness of this command is questionable
unless you also modify what the File Manager
displays about each file. For full effect, you should
either use the View All File Details command, or
select to view the file size with the View Partial
Details command.

For other sorting methods, see the Sort by Date, Sort
by Name, and Sort by Type commands.

SORT BY TYPE

File Manager

The Sort by Type command directs the File Manager
to display files within the current directory window
sorted alphabetically by filename extension.

Menu Structure

View | Sort by Type

Steps

Keyboard: ALT-V-B
Mouse: Click on View menu, then click on Sort
            by Type

Notes

This is a toggle command, meaning the command
can be turned on and off. When you select the
command, a check mark appears beside the
command on the menu. Select a different sorting
option, and the check mark disappears.

When Sort by Type is selected, the File Manager
sorts the directory displays first by filename
extension, and then by filename within extension
group. This sorting order is very handy, because it
clusters files by type. This makes it easier to work
with file commands like Copy File or Delete.

For other sorting methods, see the Sort by Date, Sort
by Name, and Sort by Size commands.

SOUND SETTINGS

Control Panel

The Sound Settings control how Windows uses
sound.

Menu Structure

Sound   Settings I Sound...

Steps

Keyboard: Alt-S-S
Mouse: Click on Settings menu, then click on
              Sound...; or double-click on the Sound
              icon

Notes

At a minimum, this command allows you to select
whether Windows should issue an audible alert
when it detects an error. However, if you have a

sound card installed in your system, this command allows you to specify different sounds to be played when different system events occur. The events to which you can attach sounds are:

Asterisk   Question
Critical Stop   Windows Exit
Default Beep   Windows Start
Exclamation

You select the event, and then assign a sound file to that event. These sound files have the file extension WAV, and are digital representations of sound that can be played on a sound card.

SPLIT

File Manager

The Split command controls the display within the current directory window.

Menu Structure

View | Split

Steps

Keyboard: Alt-V-L
Mouse: Click on View menu, then click on Split

Notes

The effect that this command has depends on the display state of the current directory window. If you have previously selected the View Tree Only or

View Directory Only commands, then the Split command will have the same effect as choosing the View Tree and Directory command; the current window is split and both the directory tree and the directory listing are shown.

On the other hand, if the current window already contains both the directory tree and directory listing, then this command allows you to change the location of the vertical border between the two sides of the window.

STATUS BAR

File Manager

The Status Bar command controls whether the status bar at the bottom of the File Manager window is displayed.

Menu Structure

Options | Status Bar

Steps

Keyboard: Alt-O-S
Mouse: Click on Options menu, then click on Status Bar

Notes

This is a toggle option that is normally enabled. A toggle option is simply one that can be turned on and off with the same command. When you select the Status Bar command the first time, the status bar at the bottom of the File Manager window disappears and the check mark beside the command on the menu disappears. Select the Status Bar command again, and the status bar and menu check mark reappear.

With the Status Bar option turned on, the File Manager can provide more detailed information about the status of your work. Normally, it is used to display a message indicating the result of the last operation. If you feel comfortable without such information, or if the status bar bothers you, then turn it off.

The use of this command is a personal preference. It does not affect the overall functioning of Windows.

SWITCH TO

System-wide

The Switch To command lets you select, end, and organize currently running tasks.

Menu Structure

Control | Switch to...

Steps

Keyboard: Alt – Spacebar – W
Shortcut: Ctrl – Esc
Mouse: Click on Control menu, then click on Switch to...

Notes

The Control menu is accessed through the icon in the upper-left corner of a window.

This command is used to switch between tasks. *Tasks* are individual programs running under Windows. When you choose this command, you are presented with a list of the currently executing tasks. You can select a task and press Enter, double-click on a task, or click on a task and click on the *Switch To* button, and that task will be switched to the foreground. You can also terminate programs using this command by selecting a task and then clicking on the *End Task* button.

You can choose the Cascade, Tile, or Arrange Icons options from this command to perform the same functions in relation to the tasks as you do when using them as individual commands.

Tips

If you are using a mouse, you can double-click on the desktop (outside of any windows) in order to access the Task List. This is the same as using the Switch To command.

TILE WINDOWS

Program Manager or File Manager

The Tile Windows command arranges the open document windows in a side-by-side fashion.

Menu Structure

Window | Tile

Steps

Keyboard: ALT-W-T
Shortcut: SHIFT-F4
Mouse: Click on Window menu, then click on Tile

Notes

If you get several windows open on your screen at once, it can quickly become cluttered. If you choose this command, Windows will, within the available desktop space, rearrange the windows so they are side-by-side with each other.

When tiling the windows, they are resized and, if Auto Arrange is enabled, the icons are rearranged in each window. The following shows a screen after tiling:

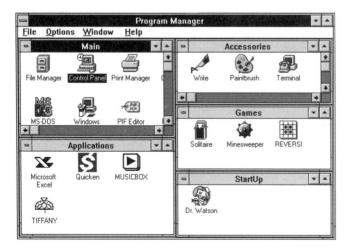

VIEW ALL FILE DETAILS

File Manager

The View All File Details command directs the File Manager to display all information about files shown in the file window.

Menu Structure

View | All File Details

Steps

Keyboard: Alt-V-A
Mouse: Click on View menu, then click on All File Details

Notes

This is a toggle command, meaning the command can be turned on and off. When you select the command, a check mark appears beside the command on the menu. Select a different viewing detail option, and the check mark disappears.

When View All File Details is selected, the File Manager displays full information on each file in a subdirectory. The information displayed includes the filename, its size, date and time of creation, and its properties. The date and time displayed for a file indicates the last time the file was *changed*, not the last time it was accessed.

The file properties display may show nothing to the right of a file entry, or there may be the letters R, H,

S, or A. These letters indicate the attributes, or *properties*, possessed by the file. Normally you won't see files with the H or S attributes displayed; this can be changed with the View By File Type command. For more information on file properties, see the Properties command.

For other display modes, see the View by Name and View Partial Details commands.

VIEW BY FILE TYPE

File Manager

The View By File Type command specifies which files should be displayed by the File Manager.

Menu Structure

View | By File Type...

Steps

Keyboard: Alt-V-T
Mouse: Click on View menu, then click on By File Type...

Notes

With the View By File Type command you can specify the name and type of files to be displayed by the File Manager. In addition, you can select whether system and hidden files are displayed.

The Name box allows you to indicate a template that will be used to determine which files get displayed. Normally, this is set to *.*, the DOS wildcard characters, which indicate that any named files should be listed. You can specify partial names or get really fancy with this parameter. Full discussion of filenames and wildcard characters is beyond the scope of this pocket reference. For more information, see *Simply DOS* or *DOS: The Complete Reference*, Third Edition, both by Kris Jamsa.

The File Type box lists the file types that can be displayed by the File Manager. You can select which ones are displayed and which ones aren't. The possibilities are

Directories   If the Directories option is selected, then directories are included in file displays.

Programs   If the Programs option is selected, then files with the EXE, COM, BAT, or PIF file extension are included in file displays.

Documents   If the Documents option is selected, then files associated with programs are displayed. See the Associate File command for more information.

Other Files   If the Other Files option is selected, nonprogram and nondocument files are included in file displays.

If you specify that system and hidden files are displayed, then they are included in file listings.

Changes with this command affect only the current File Manager window, unless you check the "Set System Default" box. Doing so causes your changes to have effect on all File Manager operations.

VIEW BY NAME

File Manager

The View by Name command directs the File Manager to display only the filenames in the file window.

Menu Structure

View | Name

Steps

Keyboard: Alt-V-N
Mouse:　　Click on View menu, then click on Name

Notes

This is a toggle command, meaning the command can be turned on and off. When you select the command, a check mark appears beside the command on the menu. Select a different viewing detail option, and the check mark disappears.

When View by Name is selected, the File Manager displays only filenames in the file window. For other viewing detail options, see the View All File Details and View Partial Details commands.

VIEW DIRECTORY ONLY

File Manager

The View Directory Only command controls the display within the current directory window.

Menu Structure

View | Directory Only

Steps

Keyboard: ALT-V-O
Mouse: Click on View menu, then click on Directory Only

Notes

This is a toggle command, meaning the command can be turned on and off. When you select the command the first time, the display in the current directory window is changed, and a check mark appears beside the command on the menu. If you use another directory window display command (View Tree and Directory or View Tree Only), the check mark moves to the other command setting.

When enabled, this option causes the File Manager to display only the directory listing within the current directory window. The left portion of the window, normally occupied by the directory tree, disappears entirely. This option is good to use where there are very many files in the current directory, and you want to see as many of them as possible.

VIEW PARTIAL DETAILS

File Manager

The View Partial Details command allows you to choose the information displayed for each file by the File Manager.

Menu Structure

View | Partial Details...

Steps

Keyboard: Alt-V-P
Mouse: Click on View menu, then click on Partial Details...

Notes

When you select View Partial Details, you can select the type of information you want the File Manager to display for each file. The available information includes

Size   The size of the file, in bytes.

Last Modification Date   The date on which the file was either created or last written to.

Last Modification Time   The time at which the file was either created or last written to.

File Attributes   The properties of the file, as fully described in the Properties command.

Your choices with the View Partial Details command
are overridden when you later select the View All
File Details or View by Name commands.

VIEW PRINT FILE SIZE

Print Manager

The View Print File Size command controls the
information displayed with pending print jobs.

Menu Structure

View | Print File Size

Steps

Keyboard: ALT-V-P
Mouse: Click on View menu, then click on Print
             File Size

Notes

This is a toggle option, meaning the same command
turns the option on and off. When you select the
command the first time, a check mark appears
beside the command on the menu, indicating it is
enabled. Select the Print File Size command again,
and the check mark disappears and the feature is
disabled.

If enabled, this command causes the Print Manager
to display the size, in bytes, of each print job that is
waiting to print. To display more information about
print jobs, see the View Time/Date Sent command.

VIEW TIME/DATE SENT

Print Manager

The View Time/Date Sent command controls the information displayed with pending print jobs.

Menu Structure

View | Time/Date Sent

Steps

Keyboard: Alt-V-T
Mouse: Click on View menu, then click on Time/
            Date Sent

Notes

This is a toggle option, meaning the same command turns the option on and off. When you select the command the first time, a check mark appears beside the command on the menu, indicating it is enabled. Select Time/Date Sent again, and the check mark disappears and the feature is disabled.

If enabled, this command causes the Print Manager to display the date and time that each print job was created. This can be helpful in remembering what is in each job. To display more information about print jobs, see the View Print File Size command.

VIEW TREE AND DIRECTORY

File Manager

The View Tree and Directory command controls the display within the current directory window.

Menu Structure

View | Tree and Directory

Steps

Keyboard: ALT-V-R
Mouse: Click on View menu, then click on Tree and Directory

Notes

This is a toggle command, meaning the command can be turned on and off. When you select the command the first time, the display in the current directory window is changed, and a check mark appears beside the command on the menu. If you use another directory window display command (View Directory Only or View Tree Only), the check mark moves to the other command setting.

When enabled, this option causes the File Manager to display both the tree and directory listings in the current directory window.

VIEW TREE ONLY

File Manager

The View Tree Only command controls the display within the current directory window.

Menu Structure

View | Tree Only

Steps

Keyboard: Alt-V-E
Mouse: Click on View menu, then click on Tree Only

Notes

This is a toggle command, meaning the command can be turned on and off. When you select the command the first time, the display in the current directory window is changed, and a check mark appears beside the command on the menu. If you use another directory window display command (View Directory Only or View Tree and Directory), the check mark moves to the other command setting.

When enabled, this option causes the File Manager to display only the directory tree in the current directory window. The directory display (normally the right side of the window) disappears entirely.

Task Reference

This section provides a quick overview of common tasks and how they are accomplished in Windows 3.1. Every attempt has been made to make the task names as short and simple as possible so you can find the operation you need to perform even if you have no idea what the command name might be.

The discussions under these tasks include the use of many commands. You can look up these commands in the Command Reference section for a full description of each.

Tasks are arranged in alphabetical order. The heading for each task is presented in the following manner:

TASK NAME

Following each heading is a question that puts the task into a context that many users might face. The purpose of these questions is to focus your own ideas about how each task could apply to your use of Windows.

Notes

Following the introductory question is the Notes category. This section gives the answer to the question in a discussion that attempts to promote a fuller understanding of solutions for the task.

Pertinent Commands

Next is a category called Pertinent Commands. These are the commands that perform the task at hand, along with the program from which the command is available. Once you know which commands perform the task you're about to undertake, you may wish to refer to the Command Reference for further information about how Windows operates in relation to that task.

Related Tasks

The next category is called Related Tasks. This cross references commands within this Task Reference. It lists other tasks that are related to the one under discussion.

Suggestions

Finally, some tasks include a category called Suggestions. These are additional pointers or tips that you may find helpful in dealing with situations where the task may apply.

For a complete list of tasks in this section, see the Contents. Since the wording used for tasks is discretionary, you might not word a task in the same manner as was chosen for this section. The following list is intended as a cross-reference of alternate wording for some tasks:

If You Want to:	See the Task:
Add a command	Adding Applications
Add a program	Adding Applications
Add a program group	Creating New Program Groups

If You Want to:	See the Task:
Build a selection set	Selecting Multiple Files
Cancel a print job	Deleting a Print Job
Change colors	Changing Desktop Colors
Change date and time	Setting the Date and Time
Change a filename	Renaming a File
Change paper orientation	Setting Paper Orientation
Change a program name	Renaming a Program
Change your keyboard	Changing Your Equipment
Change your monitor	Changing Your Equipment
Choose a printer	Changing Printers
Choose a window	Selecting Windows
Create a bootable disk	Making a System Disk
Create a selection set	Selecting Multiple Files
Create a system disk	Making a System Disk
Delete an application	Deleting a Program
Duplicate a disk	Copying a Disk
Duplicate a file	Copying a File
Duplicate a program icon	Copying a Program
End a program	Stopping a Program
Erase a file	Deleting a File
Erase a program	Deleting a Program
Exit Windows	Ending Windows
Make a bootable disk	Making a System Disk
Make a directory	Creating a Directory
Make a window bigger	Maximizing Windows *or* Changing Window Sizes
Make a window smaller	Minimizing Windows *or* Changing Window Sizes
Pick a window	Selecting Windows
Quit Windows	Ending Windows
Remove a print job	Deleting a Print Job
Set landscape mode	Setting Paper Orientation
Set portrait mode	Setting Paper Orientation

ADDING APPLICATIONS

How do I add applications to run from the Program
Manager in Windows?

Notes

There are three ways to add commands to the
Program Manager in Windows:

- Use the Set Up Applications command from
the Windows Setup program. This is perhaps
the easiest method of adding programs to
Windows.

- Add applications manually. This involves
using the New command from the Program
Manager and possibly the PIF editor. This is
the most difficult way to add applications
(and sometimes the only way).

- Use a third-party install program. This is a
common method when installing a program
written specifically for Windows 3 or 3.1. The
installation program takes care of any PIF
files, adding program items, and possibly
adding program groups. These installation
programs vary widely and depend on the
good graces of the vendor supplying your new
software.

Pertinent Commands

Set Up Applications, Windows Setup
New, Program Manager
Properties, Program Manager

Related Tasks

Creating New Program Groups
Running a Program
Stopping a Program

Suggestions

If you are installing new sofware, check with the vendor to see if they have a special installation program for Windows 3 or 3.1.

Try using the Set Up Applications command to see if it can recognize and install the software you want added.

ADDING A PRINTER

I have just purchased a new printer. How do I get it to work with Windows?

Notes

The first step in adding a printer is to connect it to your computer. Generally, it will either connect to the parallel or serial port. You will need the proper cable to do this; the place where you got your printer should be able to supply one.

Since hardware lessons and cabling diagrams are a little outside the scope of this pocket reference, if you are having problems so far you should refer to another book. *Upgrading PCs Made Easy* by Bud and Alex Aaron, published by Osborne/McGraw-Hill, is a good choice.

Once your printer is connected to your computer, go ahead and start Windows 3.1. Go to the Control Panel and select the Printers icon (see the Printer Settings command for more information). Click on the button that says Add. This will allow you to load the proper printer driver for your new printer. Scroll through the list of available printers, and select the one that most closely approximates your printer. Click on the Install button and Windows will inform you if it needs a disk from which to load the printer driver. The drivers for all the printers in the List of Printers are on the original Windows software disks.

Now that the printer driver is installed, you need to click on the Connect button. This allows you to specify the printer port used by your new printer. Select the same port to which you connected your printer earlier. When you click on OK, your printer should be ready to use with Windows. If it doesn't work, check the following:

- Is the correct printer driver loaded?
- Does the printer port in Windows match the port to which the printer is actually connected?
- Are the physical cable connections tight?

Pertinent Commands

Printer Settings, Control Panel

Related Tasks

Changing Printers
Changing the Default Printer
Removing a Printer

Suggestions

If you continue to have problems making your printer work, try printing something to it from DOS (outside of Windows). If you are able to do this, then you can assume that the problem is not with the printer itself, but in how Windows is set up to access the printer.

CHANGING THE DEFAULT PRINTER

Some of my applications only print to the default printer. How do I determine what the default printer is, and how do I change it?

Notes

Some applications will simply only print to the default printer. For instance, when you print a file from the File Manager, it is directed to the default printer.

You can determine your default printer by opening the Printers icon from the Control Panel. The default printer is listed near the upper-left corner of the dialog box. To change the default printer, double-click on one of the installed printers listed in the Installed Printers list. This should change the default printer. You can also highlight a printer name and click on the Set as Default Printer button.

Pertinent Commands

Printer Settings, Control Panel

Related Tasks

Adding a Printer
Changing Printers

CHANGING DESKTOP COLORS

How do I change the colors used by Windows?

Notes

Changing colors is an easy thing to do. To change
the colors of your desktop, open the Colors icon
from the Control Panel. There you can experiment
and see how the colors will look before you make
them permanent.

Windows comes with several color combinations
already saved (see the Color Settings command for
more information). If you are so motivated, you can
also save your favorite color combinations. That
way you can call them up again at a later date. To
save color combinations, you will need to use the
Color Palette to change the menu colors. When you
are happy with how they appear, click on the Save
Scheme button and provide a name for the color
scheme.

Pertinent Commands

Color Settings, Control Panel

CHANGING DIRECTORIES

How do I change directories?

Notes

If you are familar with DOS and understand the basics of subdirectories, this may seem a natural question to ask. Basically, when you are outside of an application program, there is no need to change directories in Windows. Once you are in a program, it is up to the program to handle making directory changes.

The most common need to change directories is within the File Manager. Here you can traverse directories quickly and easily using the Directory Tree. You change directories by simply clicking on an icon that represents the directory you want. You can also use the cursor control keys to move through the directories.

Pertinent Commands

New Window, File Manager
View Tree and Directory, File Manager
View Tree Only, File Manager

Related Tasks

Changing the Drive
Creating a Directory

Suggestions

You can open, view, and access multiple directories by simply opening the desired directories from the directory tree. You can use the New Window command to open new directory windows. These windows can be arranged on the desktop so you can quickly and easily work across directories.

CHANGING THE DRIVE

How do I change the drive?

Notes

Changing drives and *specifying* drives are two different things. There are many places where you will need to specify a drive. For instance, you specify a drive when you are adding an application and you need to include a drive name on the command line designation, or when you are installing applications using the Windows Setup program and it asks which drives should be searched.

There is generally only one place where you may need to change drives, however. That is in the File Manager. To change drives here, simply click on the icon representing the disk drive. If you have a question about what type of disk drive it is, the icons will generally let you know. The following are five types of Windows drives:

Floppy drive

Hard drive

	RAM drive
	Network drive
	CD-ROM drive

As you navigate through drives and directories, Windows will keep you informed about what is happening.

The ability to change drives while using an application depends on the application. For more information, consult the documentation for the application you are using.

Pertinent Commands

Network Connections, File Manager

Related Tasks

Changing Directories

CHANGING THE KEYBOARD REPEAT RATE

When I am typing, I find that many of the keys I press are actually appearing twice on the screen. How do I correct this?

Notes

Windows allows you to control what is called the *key repeat rate*. This is the relative length of time that you must hold down a key before it repeats.

The faster the key repeat rate, the shorter the time you have to release a key before it repeats.

If you are a slow, methodical typist, then you may need to change the key repeat rate to a slower setting. This is done by using the Keyboard Settings command from the Control Panel. When you use this command, you will be able to adjust two settings that affect the key repeat rate. Try sliding the block toward the left on the Delay Before First Repeat control. This will cause Windows to wait longer before beginning to repeat your keypresses.

Note that the key repeat rate affects all keys on your keyboard, including the cursor control keys. Thus, if you slow down the key repeat rate, the arrow keys will respond slower when you hold them down.

Pertinent Commands

Keyboard Settings, Control Panel

Related Topics

Changing Your Equipment

Suggestions

If you have the key repeat rate set at the lowest setting, and you still get double keys on the screen, you could be suffering from what is called "key bounce." This is a condition caused by your computer's keyboard, not by Windows itself. Key bounce can usually only be corrected by getting a new keyboard. If you change keyboards, you may have to change the equipment settings that Windows uses for your keyboard.

CHANGING PRINTERS

I have multiple printers attached to my system. How do I change which printer is being used?

Notes

Any answer to this question assumes you already have installed the printers and that Windows is aware that the printers are available. If not, see the related discussion under the task Adding a Printer.

There are several ways you can change which printer you want to use. The first, and most common way is with the Control Panel. Go to the Control Panel and open the Printers icon. Here you can select which printer is the current printer by clicking on the printer name in the Installed Printers list and click on OK. That's all there is to it.

The other ways to select printers depend on the application programs you are using. For instance, it is possible in Write (the Windows accessory) to use the Print Setup command on the File menu to select which printer should be used. Many other programs offer similar abilities.

Pertinent Commands

Printer Settings, Control Panel
Print Setup, Help System

Related Tasks

Adding a Printer
Changing the Default Printer

CHANGING WINDOW SIZES

How do I change the size of a window?

Notes

The easiest way to change the size of the window is with the mouse. As you move the mouse cursor near the border of the active window, you will notice that the arrow changes to a double arrow. This represents the direction in which you can move that particular border. If you move the cursor near the corner of the window, you will notice that the double arrow points diagonally. This means you can affect two of the borders at the same time.

In order to change the window size with the mouse, move the mouse cursor to the border or corner you wish to change. Then click the left mouse button and, while holding it down, drag the border to the desired position. When you let go of the button, the window is resized.

If you are using the keyboard, the process is a little more intricate. You must first choose the Size command from the Control menu, and then press an arrow key to designate which border you wish to move. If you want to move a corner, you can press two arrow keys simultaneously.

Once you have selected a border or corner to move, use the arrow keys to move it. When you are satisfied with the new position, press ENTER. If you change your mind and don't want to resize the window, press ESC.

You also need to be aware that certain commands
change the size of the windows automatically. For
instance, the Tile Windows or Cascade Windows
commands affect all the windows on the screen.

Pertinent Commands

Cascade Windows, Program Manager *or* File
   Manager
Size Window, System-wide
Switch To, System-wide
Tile Windows, Program Manager *or* File Manager

CHANGING YOUR EQUIPMENT

I've just added a new piece of equipment that I
want to use with Windows. How do I do this?

Notes

There are many pieces of equipment that you can
take advantage of with Windows. These include
monitors, hard drives, printers, modems, mice,
networks, keyboards, and the like. Actually, if you
change monitors, there is nothing you need to do in
relation to Windows; the change comes in if you
change the type of display card you are using_for
instance, if you upgrade from an EGA card to a VGA
card.

If you are changing your display card, keyboard,
mouse, or network, use the Change System Settings
command to make Windows aware of your new
equipment.

If you have added an additional hard drive or a new modem, there is nothing you have to do in relation to Windows itself. Windows should automatically recognize the hard drive. You may need to make changes in your application programs, however, as these exert further control over these types of devices.

If you are changing or adding a printer, you can use the Printer Settings command. For more information on this, see the Adding a Printer task.

Pertinent Commands

Change System Settings, Windows Setup
Printer Settings, Control Panel

Related Tasks

Adding a Printer

Suggestions

If you are changing your display system to an older type (for instance, from VGA to EGA), make sure you make your display changes in Windows *before* you actually change the hardware. If you don't, you won't be able to use Windows. The VGA video drivers used by Windows will not work with EGA displays.

COPYING A DISK

I want to copy a disk. How do I do it?

Notes

How you copy a disk depends, in large part, on what you are copying *from* and *to*. If you are copying between disks that have the same capacity, you can use any of the following methods:

˘ Within the File Manager, use the Copy Disk command.

˘ Within the File Manager, use the Format Disk command to format a blank disk, and then use the Copy File command to copy the files to the new disk.

˘ From the DOS prompt, use the DISKCOPY command. This is a DOS command, and beyond the scope of this pocket reference. But access to the command is available from Windows. For more information on this command, refer to *DOS: The Complete Reference*, Third Edition, by Kris Jamsa, published by Osborne/McGraw-Hill.

If you need to copy between disks that have differing capacities, then only the second option can be used.

Pertinent Commands

Copy Disk, File Manager
Copy File, File Manager
Format Disk, File Manager

Related Tasks

Copying a File
Formatting a Disk

Suggestions

Make sure that the disk onto which you will be copying is blank. The copy commands (particularly those that copy an entire disk) are destructive in nature. This means that files on the destination disk could be overwritten by the operation.

COPYING A FILE

How do I copy my spreadsheet file to disk?

Notes

Copying a file is a simple process, whether you are copying to another directory, another hard disk, or a floppy disk. All the file copying capabilities of Windows lie within the File Manager.

Once in the File Manager, select the file or files you wish to copy. Then, use the Copy File command to specify where you want to copy the files. If you are using a mouse, open both the source and destination directories as individual windows. Then you can drag the files to be copied to their new location.

If you are not using a mouse, you must use the Copy File command and enter the complete path for the destination of the files to be copied. While this may sound difficult, it is pretty easy as long as you have a firm handle on where the files should end up.

Pertinent Commands

Copy File, File Manager
Format Disk, File Manager
Search for Files, File Manager
Select Files, File Manager

Related Tasks

Copying a Disk
Copying a Program
Formatting a Disk
Moving a File
Searching for Files
Selecting Multiple Files

Suggestions

If you are copying to a floppy disk, make sure it is
formatted before you start. You cannot copy files to
a disk that has not been formatted.

Suppose your file copying needs are as follows:

1.   There are at least two files to be copied.

2.   The files are in different subdirectories.

3.   All the files have the same extension (the
     characters in the filename following the
     period).

This is not an unusual scenario. If you find yourself
in this situation, use the Search for Files command
to build a selection set of the files that have the
common extension. Then use the Select Files
command to select all those files, and finally the
Copy File command to copy these to the destination.

COPYING A PROGRAM

How do I copy a program in one window of the Program Manager to another?

Notes

Copying a program is similar to copying a file, except all operations occur in the Program Manager. First, you need to select the program icon you wish to copy. Then, use the Copy command to specify the program group that you want to copy the program to. If you are using a mouse, open both the source and destination program groups as individual windows. Then, while holding down the Ctrl key, you can drag the icon to be copied to its new location.

If you are not using a mouse, you must use the Copy command and enter the name of the program group to receive the copy. If you can't remember the names of all the program groups, you can browse through them by clicking on the arrow at the right of the default group.

Pertinent Commands

Copy Program Item, Program Manager

Related Tasks

Copying a File
Moving a Program

CREATING A DIRECTORY

How do I add a new directory on my hard drive?

Notes

Adding a new directory is a common occurrence in DOS computing. To do this, you use the Create Directory command in the File Manager. When you use this command, you will be prompted for the name of the directory to add. Names should follow the same rules as names for files; they should be eight characters or less with up to three characters for an extension. The extension should be separated from the rest of the filename by a period. If you don't want the directory to be added within the current directory, you must provide a complete path name of the directory to add.

Pertinent Commands

Create Directory, File Manager

CREATING NEW PROGRAM GROUPS

I don't like the way some of my programs are grouped in the Program Manager. How do I create new groups and add programs to them?

Notes

Creating new program groups in the Program Manager is quite easy. You can use the New command from the Program Manager to do this.

When you issue the command, make sure you then specify that you are adding a program group.

You can give program groups any name you wish. However, your desktop will appear less cluttered if you keep each name relatively short. (The words under the program group icons tend to run together if the names are too long.)

Once you have provided a description for the new group, press ENTER. That's it. You have just added a new program group. At this point it will appear as an open window, and you can move applications into it as you please by dragging icons from other program groups. Remember to hold down the CTRL key if you want to copy icons to the new program group.

Pertinent Commands

New, Program Manager
Properties, Program Manager

Related Tasks

Adding Applications

Suggestions

If you would rather change the title of a current program group, you can use the Properties command. This eliminates the need to add a group, transfer all the files into it, and then delete the old group.

DELETING A FILE

I've been wanting to free up some disk space lately, but don't know how to delete my old files. How do I do this?

Notes

Deleting files is a common occurrence. There are a couple of ways to do it with Windows.

First, you can use the File Manager's Delete command. This allows you to delete one or more files, or an entire subdirectory. All you need to do is select the files or directories you wish to delete, and then either invoke the Delete command or, better yet, press the DEL key. Windows will make sure you really want to delete the files before continuing.

If you would rather not see the promptings before each file is deleted, use the Confirmation Options command to change this.

You may not be able to delete some of your files. If you have files with the read-only, system, or hidden attributes enabled, you won't be able to delete them. If you do want to delete them, use the Properties command (within the File Manager) to disable all the attributes of the file before trying to delete it.

Second, if you simply want to delete a program icon or a program group from the Program Manager, you need to use the Delete command within the Program Manager. It does not really erase files from the disk; it simply removes the icon associated with the program or program group from the desktop.

Pertinent Commands

Properties, File Manager
Confirmation Options, File Manager
Delete, File Manager
Delete, Program Manager

Related Tasks

Deleting a Program
Selecting Multiple Files

DELETING A PRINT JOB

I have been sending files to a nonexistent printer for
a few hours without realizing it. I think they may
still be in the Print Manager waiting to print. How
do I check this, and then delete them?

Notes

The Print Manager is a spooling program; it is a
utility that helps you manage what you want to
print. When you open the Print Manager icon, you
will be shown a list of jobs waiting to print. Each of
these jobs is either saved in your computer's
memory or on your computer's hard disk.

If you want to delete one of the jobs you see listed,
select the job and click on the Delete button. If you
are not using a mouse, select the job and press
Aʟᴛ-D. The job will be deleted and not printed.

You should also make sure that the Alert Status,
accessed through the Print Manager, is set to a

choice that will alert you when errors exist (like nonexistent or nonresponsive printers).

Pertinent Commands

Alert Always, Print Manager
Flash if Inactive, Print Manager
Ignore if Inactive, Print Manager

Related Tasks

Pausing a Print Job
Resuming a Print Job

DELETING A PROGRAM

How do I delete a program that appears on my desktop?

Notes

This is a two-step process. First, you must delete the program (or program group) using the Delete command within the Program Manager. This command does not really remove the program files from the disk, however. It simply removes the icon associated with the program or program group from the desktop.

After you have deleted the icon, open the File Manager and use the Delete command to delete the actual program files. Make sure you know which files to delete. There is no clear-cut guideline for this; you just have to do some research to discover which files are used by the program you want to delete.

The Delete command allows you to delete one or more files, or an entire subdirectory. All you need to do is select the files or directories you wish to delete, and then either invoke the Delete command or press the Dᴇʟ key.

Pertinent Commands

Delete, File Manager
Delete, Program Manager

Related Tasks

Deleting a File

Suggestions

For a shortcut, you can also remove a program or program group from the desktop by selecting it and pressing the Dᴇʟ key.

ENDING WINDOWS

How do I get out of Windows?

Notes

There are four ways to end your Windows session:

1. Double-click on the Control Menu icon for the Program Manager window.

2. With the Program Manager active, use the Close Window command (accessed by pressing Aʟᴛ-F4).

3. Use the Exit Windows command from the Program Manager.

4. From the Task List (accessed with the Switch To command) choose the Program Manager and click on the End Task button.

Before you end Windows, make sure all your applications have been ended and the appropriate data files are closed.

It is a good idea to never end Windows by simply turning off your computer. This can lead to later problems with your programs if they are processing data when the computer is turned off.

Pertinent Commands

Close Window, System-wide
Exit Windows, Program Manager
Switch To, System-wide

FORMATTING A DISK

How do I format a disk?

Notes

If you want to format a floppy disk, use the Format Disk command from within the File Manager. This will allow you to format a floppy disk in any drive that uses the floppy drive icon, shown here:

If you want the disk to be bootable, once you choose the Format Disk command, choose the Make System Disk option.

If you want to format a hard drive, you will have to do so from the DOS prompt. Windows does not allow you to format hard drives.

Pertinent Commands

Format Disk, File Manager

Suggestions

Make sure the disk you want to format is blank. Format Disk is a destructive command; it will erase any data on the floppy disk being formatted.

GETTING HELP

When I'm working with Windows, I often need a little help. Is there a fast way I can get it?

Notes

Help is only a keypress away (or so the saying goes). Windows 3.1 has a full-featured Help System that you can even expand with your own input. You can access the Help System at any time by simply using the pull-down Help menu, or by pressing F1.

Pertinent Commands

Annotate, Help System
Copy, Help System
Define Bookmark, Help System

Open File, Help System
Print Topic, Help System
Print Setup, Help System

Suggestions

If you find yourself referring to the same help sections again and again, you may want to define a few bookmarks using the Define Bookmark command to make finding that troublesome command easier.

MAKING A SYSTEM DISK

I need a floppy disk that I can use to boot another system. Is there anything special I have to do, other than to format the disk?

Notes

Formatting a disk only prepares it to hold information. It organizes the disk and sets up the structure used by DOS and Windows. If you want to make a disk bootable, you need to create a system disk. This is a disk that has special system files on it. These files contain DOS and enable a computer to complete the booting process.

There are two ways to make a system disk. The first is to place the special system files on the disk as it is formatted. This is done if you select the Make System Disk option when you use the Format Disk command. The other method uses the Make System Disk command, and assumes you have previously formatted the disk. Refer to the appropriate sections of the Command Reference for more information on these commands.

Pertinent Commands

Format Disk, File Manager
Make System Disk, File Manager

Related Tasks

Formatting a Disk

MAXIMIZING WINDOWS

I am having a hard time reading the application window I am using. How do I make it larger?

Notes

There are two ways to make windows larger. The first is to change the window size, which is done by adjusting the window borders. For more information on this, see the task Changing Window Sizes.

The other method is to *maximize* the window. This makes it as large as possible, usually covering the entire screen. This is done in one of two ways:

- If you are using a mouse, click on the maximize button. This is a button with an upward-pointing arrow, located in the upper-right corner of the window.

- If you are not using a mouse, use the Maximize Window command.

Either method will maximize the window, and should cure any problems brought about by having a workspace that is too small.

Pertinent Commands

Maximize Window, System-wide

Related Tasks

Changing Window Sizes
Minimizing Windows

MINIMIZING WINDOWS

My desktop is getting cluttered. How do I shrink some open windows so they are as small as possible?

Notes

There are two ways to make windows smaller. The first is to change the window size, which is done by moving the window borders. For more information on this, see the task Changing Window Sizes.

The other method (and the one more appropriate to the question) is to *minimize* the window. This makes it as small as possible, shrinking the window to a single icon. This is done in one of two ways:

˘ If you are using a mouse, click on the minimize button. This is a button with a downward-pointing arrow, located in the upper-right corner of the window.

˘ If you are not using a mouse, use the
  Minimize Window command.

Pertinent Commands

Minimize on Use, Program Manager *or* File
  Manager
Minimize Window, System-wide

Suggestions

You can use the Minimize on Use command within
the Program Manager or File Manager to cause
these programs to minimize automatically when you
run an application from them.

MOVING A FILE

How do I move a file from one directory to another?

Notes

Moving files is similar to copying them. In fact,
moving is nothing more than copying and then
deleting the original. You move files from within
the File Manager.

Once in the File Manager, select the file or files you
wish to move. Then, use the Move File command to
specify where you want to move them. If you are
using a mouse, open both the source and
destination directories as individual windows.
Then you can drag the files to be moved to their
new location.

If you are not using a mouse, you must use the
Move File command and enter the complete path for
the destination of the files to be moved. While this
may sound more difficult, it is pretty easy as long as
you have a firm handle on where the files should
end up.

Pertinent Commands

Copy File, File Manager
Move, Program Manager
Move File, File Manager

Related Tasks

Copying a File
Formatting a Disk
Moving a Program
Selecting Multiple Files

Suggestions

If you are moving files to a floppy disk, make sure it
is formatted first. You cannot store information on
an unformatted disk.

MOVING A PROGRAM

How do I move a program from one window of the
Program Manager to another?

Notes

Moving a program is similar to moving a file, except
all operations occur in the Program Manager.

First, you need to select the program icon you wish to move. If you are using a mouse, open the source program group. Then drag the icon to its new location. This location can be either another open program group window, or a program group icon.

If you are not using a mouse, you must use the Move command and enter the name of the program group to which the program should be moved. If you can't remember the names of all the program groups, you can browse through them by clicking on the arrow at the right of the default group.

Pertinent Commands

Move, Program Manager

Related Tasks

Copying a Program
Moving a File

PAUSING A PRINT JOB

I am using the Print Manager, but want to pause the file I have just printed so that I can make some printer adjustments. How do I do this?

Notes

The Print Manager is a spooling program; it is a utility that helps you manage what you want to print. When you open the Print Manager icon, you will be shown a list of jobs waiting to print, as well as printers that the Print Manager recognizes.

If you want to pause what is going to one of the printers, select the printer and click on the Pause button. If you are not using a mouse, select the printer and press Aʟᴛ-P. A small icon will appear to the left of the printer line, and nothing will be sent to the printer until you choose to resume printing.

Related Tasks

Deleting a Print Job
Resuming a Print Job

PRINTING

OK, I give up! How do I print?

Notes

For some strange reason, in Windows you can usually find the printer-related commands listed under the File menu. Before you can choose the Print command (this sends the actual output to your printer), there are a few steps you must do:

1. Make sure you have installed the correct printer drivers. See the Adding a Printer task for more information.

2. Make sure you have selected the right hardware port for the printer.

3. Make sure you have configured and set up the printer correctly.

4. Make sure the printer is turned on, online, and available for use.

5. If you are using the Print Manager, make sure that output to the printer is not paused.

6. Make sure your information is formatted in the desired fashion. (This is entirely dependant on the application program you are using.)

If you do all these things, you should be able to get your output using the Print command.

Pertinent Commands

Alert Always, Print Manager
Change System Settings, Windows Setup
Flash if Inactive, Print Manager
High Priority, Print Manager
Ignore if Inactive, Print Manager
Low Priority, Print Manager
Medium Priority, Print Manager
Print File, File Manager
Print Topic, Help System
Printer Settings, Control Panel
Print Setup, Help System

Related Tasks

Adding a Printer
Changing Printers
Changing the Default Printer
Pausing a Print Job
Resuming a Print Job
Setting Paper Orientation

Suggestions

The first time you use Windows with a printer or the first time you use a new printer with Windows, make sure you are not rushed. Give yourself plenty of time to get used to the new system and comfortable with its capabilities.

REMOVING A PRINTER

I have upgraded my printer, and I successfully added the new printer driver to Windows. How do I delete the old printer driver, since I don't need it any more?

Notes

Removing a printer driver is a much easier process than adding a printer. To remove a printer, open the Printers icon from the Control Panel. From the Installed Printers list, select the printer to be removed, and then click on the Remove button. Windows will ask you to confirm your action; if you do so, the printer driver is removed from the list of installed printers.

The printer drivers you have removed will not really be removed until you click the OK button on the Printers dialog box. If you click on Cancel, or press Esc, the removal is not completed.

If you later decide you wish to add the printer driver, you will have to go through the process of adding a printer again.

Pertinent Commands

Printer Settings, Control Panel

Related Tasks

Adding a Printer
Changing Printers
Changing the Default Printer

Suggestions

Keeping the old printer driver installed does not hurt anything. You may want to simply configure it so that output for that printer goes to a file. That way, if you ever get visiting rights for your old printer, you will still be able to print a file through it.

RENAMING A FILE

How do I change the name of a file?

Notes

If you want to change the name of a program file in the Program Manager, see the task Renaming a Program.

You can change filenames using the File Manager. This is done with the Rename command. Actually, you can use this command to rename directories or files. There are only a few conditions under which you cannot do a rename:

˘   You cannot rename the root directory of a drive.

˘   You cannot rename a file that has the read-only file attribute enabled.

˘ You cannot rename a file or directory to a
name already in use by another file in the
same directory.

When you use the Rename command, you are
shown the old name of the file or directory, and
asked to enter a new name. Names should follow
the standard rules for files; they should be eight
characters or less with up to three characters for an
extension. The extension should be separated from
the rest of the filename by a period. You cannot
enter a disk drive designation in the new name. If
you do, you will get an error message.

Pertinent Commands

Rename, File Manager

Related Tasks

Copying a File
Creating a Directory
Deleting a File
Moving a File
Renaming a Program

Suggestions

Be careful in renaming files and directories. If you
rename program files that are used elsewhere in
Windows, then Windows will not be able to find the
program unless you make additional changes. If
you change the name of data files needed by
application programs, it is possible those programs
will not be able to function properly because
Windows is not able to find the data files.

RENAMING A PROGRAM

How do I rename a program shown in the Program Manager?

Notes

Renaming programs in the Program Manager is really quite simple. The name shown under the program icon and at the top of the application window is completely under your control.

To change the program name, select the program icon whose name you wish to change. Then use the Properties command and change the description line. That's it.

Pertinent Commands

Properties, Program Manager

Related Tasks

Adding Applications
Deleting a Program
Renaming a File

Suggestions

Windows comes with program names that are good for general purposes, but if you would rather see different names, then change them. This will have no affect on anything else you do in Windows.

RESUMING A PRINT JOB

I am using the Print Manager, and I previously
paused output to a printer. How do I resume
printing my files?

Notes

The Print Manager is a spooling program; it is a
utility that helps you manage what you want to
print. When you open the Print Manager icon, you
will be shown a list of jobs waiting to print, as well
as printers that the Print Manager recognizes. If a
printer has been paused, a small icon will appear to
the left of the printer line.

To resume printing to a printer, select one that has
been paused (it has the icon), and click on the
Resume button. If you are not using a mouse, select
the printer and press ALT-R. Information should
start flowing to the printer right away.

Related Tasks

Deleting a Print Job
Pausing a Print Job

RUNNING A PROGRAM

How do I run a program from Windows?

Notes

There are several ways to run programs within Windows:

- Use the Run command from either the Program Manager or File Manager. When you choose this, you must provide the program name and any parameters necessary to run the program.

- Select the icon for the program you want to run, and then issue the Open command.

- If you are using a mouse, double-click on the icon for the program you want to run. This can be either a program item icon (in the Program Manager) or an icon for an EXE, COM, BAT, or PIF file in the File Manager.

- In the File Manager, select a file that has been attached to a program. Open the file.

- If you are using a mouse and are in the File Manager, drag the icon for a data file onto the top of the program icon.

Regardless of the method used, the effect is still the same. Windows attempts to load the file and execute the program.

If you attempt to open a non-Windows program, it is possible that it will not run in the Windows environment. If you find this is the case, you may be able to solve the problem through the use of PIF files for the application. Creating, maintaining, and using PIF files is beyond the scope of this pocket reference. For more information, refer to *Windows 3.1: The Complete Reference* by Tom Sheldon.

Pertinent Commands

Open, Program Manager or File Manager
Run, Program Manager or File Manager

Related Tasks

Stopping a Program

SEARCHING FOR FILES

I have so many files on my hard drive, I find it
virtually impossible to remember where they all are.
How do I find files on my hard drive?

Notes

You can search for files from within the File
Manager. Use the Search for Files command to look
for files either in the current directory or across the
entire disk.

Before you use the Search for Files command, make
sure you have selected the disk drive you wish to
search. After you select the command, you are
prompted for the file specification to use when
searching. You can specify partial names or get
really fancy with this parameter. Full discussion of
filenames and wildcard characters is beyond the
scope of this pocket reference. For more
information, see *Simply DOS* or *DOS: The Complete
Reference*, Third Edition, both by Kris Jamsa.

If you want to search the entire disk, indicate the
search is to start at the root directory, and select the
Search All Subdirectories option. When you press

ENTER or click on the OK button, the File Manager will compile a list of files that match your specification. These are presented in the Search Results window.

Pertinent Commands

Search for Files, File Manager

Related Tasks

Selecting Multiple Files

SELECTING MULTIPLE FILES

I need to delete a group of files. How do I select a group of files?

Notes

Typically, the File Manager only acts on the highlighted file. You can select multiple files, which is referred to as building a selection set, in any of several ways.

- If you are entering a filename when prompted by a command, you can use DOS wildcard characters. Full discussion of wildcard characters is beyond the scope of this pocket reference. For more information, see *Simply DOS* or *DOS: The Complete Reference*, Third Edition, both by Kris Jamsa and published by Osborne/McGraw-Hill.

- If you are using a mouse, you can click on the first filename you want in the selection set. Then, while holding down the SHIFT key, click on the last filename for the selection set. All files between the first and last filenames will be highlighted.

˘ If you are using a mouse, you can hold down the Ctrl key and click on the files you want in the selection set. Each file you click on is highlighted and added to the selection set.

˘ Use the Select Files command to select files in the current window.

˘ Use the Search for Files command to create a window that lists files based on your specific search criteria. Then you can use any method previously listed to build your selection set.

Pertinent Commands

Select Files, File Manager
Search for Files, File Manger

Related Tasks

Searching for Files

SELECTING WINDOWS

How do I choose the active window?

Notes

If you are using a mouse, you can choose the active window simply by clicking on the left mouse button anywhere within a window.

If you are not using a mouse, the process is a little more complex. You can use any of the following control keys:

CTRL-F6 Selects the next document window or icon in the current application window.

CTRL-TAB Same as CTRL-F6; selects the next document window or icon in the current application window.

CTRL-SHIFT-TAB This does the reverse of CTRL-TAB; cycles through the document windows and icons in reverse order in the current applications window.

CTRL-ESC Displays the Task List window, from which you can select among the currently open application windows.

ALT-ESC Selects the next application window.

If you are working solely with document windows, you can also use the Next Window command from the Control menu. This will cause the next document window to become active.

Pertinent Commands

Next Window, System-wide

Related Tasks

Changing Window Sizes
Maximizing Windows
Minimizing Windows

SETTING THE DATE AND TIME

Daylight savings time has just kicked in, and I need to change the time on my computer. How do I do this?

Notes

Your computer system keeps track of the time and date internally. Windows accesses this information in order to control some functions. For instance, the Calendar accessory uses the date and time information to operate properly.

Changing the date and time is a simple task. All you need to do is open the Date/Time icon on the Control Panel. You will see a display of both the date and time, which you can modify either by typing in new information, or by using the up and down control buttons to change it.

If you want to change the format in which the date and time are displayed, you can use the International Settings command.

Pertinent Commands

Date & Time Settings, Control Panel
International Settings, Control Panel

Suggestions

If you only have to change the time by a single hour, highlight the hour in the Time box, and click on the upward- or downward-pointing arrow. This causes the time to increase or decrease by one hour.

SETTING PAPER ORIENTATION

I have one of these fancy laser printers. How do I
make my file print sideways on the paper?

Notes

There are two ways to orient text and graphics on a
piece of paper. These are called *portrait orientation*
and *landscape orientation*. The following illustrates
the difference between the two:

Portrait orientation has the text or pictures running
parallel to the short side of the paper just like a
portrait in an art gallery; landscape has them
running parallel to the long side.

For laser printers you can change the orientation of
your paper through the Printer Settings command.
Open the Printers icon within the Control Panel.
Then, from the Installed Printers list select the
printer you are going to use and click on the Setup
button.

If Windows is capable of controlling the paper
orientation of your printer, you will see a place to
set this in the lower-left corner of the dialog box.
Select whether you want portrait or landscape

orientation. Click on the OK button and then use the Close button, and you are ready to begin printing.

It is also possible that some application programs allow you to change paper orientation. For instance, you can change orientation from the Write accessory, or with the Print Setup command of the Help System.

Pertinent Commands

Printer Settings, Control Panel
Print Setup, Help System

Related Tasks

Adding a Printer
Changing Printers
Changing the Default Printer

Suggestions

If you print a variety of documents with your printer, don't forget to change the paper orientation before each printing.

STOPPING A PROGRAM

How do I stop an application?

Notes

There are several ways to stop an application. These include

  ˘ Choose Exit from within the application. This
     command can usually be found under the File
     menu.

  ˘ If you are using a mouse, double-click on the
     Control Menu icon.

  ˘ Use the Close Window command.

  ˘ Use the Switch To command to pull up the
     Task List. Select the application you want to
     end, and then select the End Task button.

Any of these choices will effectively do the same
thing. Select the method you are most comfortable
with.

Pertinent Commands

  Close Window, System-wide
  Switch To, System-wide

Related Tasks

  Running a Program

USING THE CLIPBOARD

How do I use the Clipboard?

Notes

The Clipboard is an integral part of virtually every
application program written for Windows. It is the
Clipboard that allows you to Cut, Copy, and Paste.

When you use the Cut or Copy editing commands
available on the Edit menu of most application

programs, the information you have selected, whether it is text or graphics, is copied into the Clipboard. Whatever was in the Clipboard before is lost; only the most recent Cut or Copy is retained. Later, when you use the Paste command, the information in the Clipboard is inserted at the location of your cursor.

When you quit your application program, the contents of the Clipboard are not disturbed. You can then start another program and paste the old Clipboard information into a document in that program.

Besides using the Clipboard with application software, you can actually open the Clipboard and operate on it directly. The Clipboard is available as a program within the Program Manager.

When you open the Clipboard icon, you are shown what it contains. You can then use a variety of commands (all available from the Clipboard menu) to process the information in the Clipboard.

Pertinent Commands

Delete Clipboard, Clipboard
Open Clipboard File, Clipboard
Save As, Clipboard

USING THE TASK LIST

What is the Task List, and how do I use it?

Notes

The Task List is an internal list, maintained by
Windows, of all applications currently running.
Tasks are individual programs running under
Windows. The Task List is the main switching
point for applications running at the same time.

To access the Task List, use the Switch To
command. This is available from the Control menu
in an application window, or you can call it up by
pressing Ctrl-Esc. If you are using a mouse, you can
double-click anywhere on the desktop (outside of
any open window). The following is an example of
a Task List:

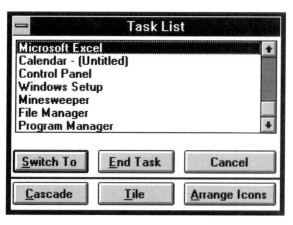

Notice the full list of currently open applications.
You can select a task and press Enter, double-click
on a task, or click on a task and click on the Switch
To button, and that task will be switched to the
foreground. You can also terminate programs using
this command by selecting a task and then clicking
on the End Task button.

The bottom three buttons on the Task List window are for arranging application windows and icons. You can experiment with them if you want to see what effect they will have on your desktop. They will not affect how the programs run.

Pertinent Commands

Switch To, System-wide

Related Tasks

Running a Program
Stopping a Program

Index